Albert

Prince Albert
His life and work

Prince Albert : His life and work

HERMIONE HOBHOUSE

Published by
HAMISH HAMILTON LIMITED
in conjunction with
THE OBSERVER
Midland Bank Group
The Royal College of Art

First published in Great Britain in 1983
by Hamish Hamilton Ltd
Garden House, 57–59 Long Acre,
London WC2E 9JZ

Published to coincide with the Exhibition,
Prince Albert: His Life and Work, held at the
Royal College of Art, London, in 1983/1984
and sponsored by THE OBSERVER with
Midland Bank Group.

Advisory Committee for the Exhibition:

Patron
H.R.H. The Duke of Edinburgh, K.G. K.T.

Chairman
Sir Hugh Casson, K.C.V.O. P.R.A.

H.H. Prince Friedrich Josias of Saxe-Coburg
and Gotha
Geoffrey de Bellaigue, C.V.O. F.S.A.
Russell Brown, F.C.A.
The Right Hon. Paul Channon, M.P.
The Lord Flowers, F.R.S.
J. D. Greenwell, F.I.B.
Sir George Howard
Ian Hunter, M.B.E.
C. A. H. James
Robert Rhodes James, M.P.
Sir Kirby Laing, J.P. M.A. F.Eng. D.L.
Sir Robin Mackworth-Young, K.C.V.O. F.S.A.
Sir Oliver Millar, K.C.V.O. F.B.A. F.S.A.
Brian Nicholson
Peter Rumble
Sir Roy Strong, Ph.D. F.S.A.
Sir David Willcocks, C.B.E. M.C.

The author and publishers thank the Royal
College of Art for their help in assembling
the illustrations for this book.

Designer of the Exhibition: Nicholas Jenkins
Designer of the book: Roger Davies

Available in hardback
ISBN 0-241-11142-0
and in paperback at the site of the
exhibition only
ISBN 0-241-11149-8

Phototypeset by Oliver Burridge & Co. Ltd
Printed and bound in Great Britain by
Billing & Sons Ltd, Worcester

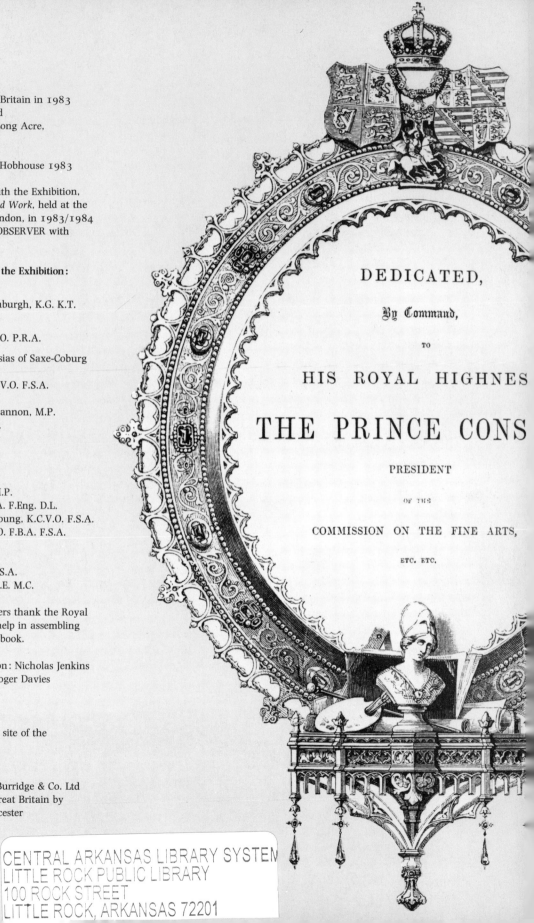

DEDICATED,

By Command,

TO

HIS ROYAL HIGHNES

THE PRINCE CONS

PRESIDENT

OF THE

COMMISSION ON THE FINE ARTS,

ETC. ETC.

Contents

DESIGNED FOR THE  **GREAT EXHIBITION.**

LONDON.

J. Wilde and Sons.

Foreword

H.R.H.
the
Duke of Edinburgh
K.G., K.T.

'I conceive it to be the duty of every educated person closely to watch and study the time in which he lives, and, as far as in him lies, to add his humble mite of individual exertion to further the accomplishment of what he believes Providence to have ordained.'

This exhibition shows that no-one fulfilled his duty in greater measure than the author of these words, Prince Albert himself. It has never been possible to assess the full and lasting value of 'individual exertion' during the lifetime or immediately after the death of a famous person. It requires patient scholarship and the winnowing action of the years to put that exertion into perspective.

Prince Albert was certainly recognized in his own time for a wide variety of accomplishments but it is only in recent years that the full range of his contribution to British national life has begun to emerge. I am sure this exhibition will provide a great deal of pleasure and interest and also enhance Prince Albert's already considerable reputation.

Buckingham Palace
1983

Introduction

'With Prince Albert we have buried our sovereign,' declared Disraeli in 1862. 'This German Prince has governed England for twenty-one years with a wisdom and energy such as none of our kings have ever shown.' Disraeli's comment was made soon after the Prince's death, subsequent commentators have on the whole endorsed his opinion.

The Exhibition, which this book commemorates, concentrates on Prince Albert's work for education, art and science, treating him less perhaps as a 'sovereign' than as a Minister for the Arts *avant la lettre*. It is, of course, impossible to ignore his role as husband of the Queen, and the enormous effect of an organized and methodical figure at the Queen's elbow for more than twenty years, 'a guiding hand, whose influence was all the greater because it never came prominently before the eyes of men'.[1] His great contribution in this role as the Queen's secretary was to free the British monarchy from the party allegiances which had hitherto been accepted, to pave the way for a constitutional model in which there was a place for Her Majesty's Opposition as much as for Her Majesty's Government.

The way to illustrate this was, I felt, the re-creation of the Prince's study, and this we have done, using for evidence the coloured photograph of his study reproduced on page 37, and the inventory of the room from the Royal Archives. Evidence of his industry can be found in the Archives themselves in his papers, carefully filed according to a system invented by the Prince himself, often annotated or even drafted in his own hand.

In other areas, there is an embarrassing amount of material. Prince Albert's most tangible monuments are perhaps the Royal palaces which were built in his lifetime: Osborne, Buckingham Palace, and Balmoral; his farm buildings at Windsor, both aesthetic and practical; his collections of paintings, of prints and drawings. These were not, however, just the relaxations of a dilettante building owner — the palaces were convenient and healthy homes for his large family. The farms, as 'Albert the Farmer' never ceased to point out to British agricultural interests, were up-to-date in pedigree livestock, machinery and accounting methods, and provided an opportunity to put into practice in dealing with employees the humane principles of the philanthropic organizations of which the Prince was patron. Similarly, in the artistic field, his interests were not those of a mere fashionable collector, though his means were probably

The First of May 1851 by F. X. Winterhalter: the old Duke of Wellington is shown with the Queen, the Prince and Arthur, later Duke of Connaught, his godson. The Crystal Palace for the 1851 Exhibition can be seen in the background.

smaller than those of many contemporaries. His collecting of early German and Italian pictures was *avante garde*, he cooperated wholeheartedly over the publications of engravings of many works of art in the Royal collections, while the work he put in hand on the Raphael archive is a most interesting prototype of modern comparative scholarship.

There was, of course, a lighter side to Court life, and a section of the Exhibition has been dedicated to this, to the family occasions, the balls, the sporting expeditions, which provided such a necessary antidote to long hours in committees and at his desk. Even the Court balls had their serious side — sometimes they were used to encourage a depressed textile industry, sometimes to entertain difficult foreign visitors.

He lived through the Crimean War and, though his work on foreign policy and foreign affairs does not fit easily into the Exhibition, his work for the British Army deserves a section to itself. His interest in the improvement of clothing, weapons and equipment, his concern for the better education of officers, and in the training of both officers and men rendered the British Army invaluable service.

For his most lasting memorial we must turn to the 1851 Exhibition and its aftermath, the creation of Albertopolis, the South Kensington complex of museums and colleges. One section of the Exhibition commemorates the exhibitions themselves, not only the 'Great Exhibition of 1851' but also the three successors, almost as important to the understanding of the Prince's ideas on practical art and science. These were the Dublin Exhibition of 1853, the Manchester Art Treasures Exhibition of 1857, and the London International Exhibition of 1862. The land at South Kensington was purchased out of the profits from the Great Exhibition, and this was laid out according to the Prince's ideas for the promotion of applied art and practical scientific education.

Most difficult of all to convey in such an exhibition is the partnership with the Queen. There were stormy moments, differences in temperament — the young Queen was fond of late nights, the Prince was always an early riser — and Queen Victoria could complain to her eldest daughter that 'Papa has his faults too. He is often very trying in his hastiness and over-love of business . . .'[2] But there was also the Prince's tactful help with the many boxes, the discreet drafting of replies to Ministers, the easing of what would have been an intolerable load for any one person, and the Queen's enthusiasm for his ideas, his collecting, his public appearances. The effect on the Queen of his sudden death was traumatic, leaving her psychologically and indeed practically unsupported. The many portraits with the ever-present bust, the commemorative pictures, the preoccupation with statues and memorials, symbolize the importance attached by the Queen to the memory of the 'beloved Prince'.

Posterity has been less understanding of Prince Albert than his immediate contemporaries who, even if they did not warm to him personally, appreciated the work that he was doing and lamented his early death. The Prince's very anxiety not to put a foot wrong made him stiff in his manner, while the patronizing attitude of many of the English grandees about the Court must have made life difficult for the young foreigner. On the other hand, his real and informed interest in any technical matter made him the friend and often the hero of humbler people. There are not many young men of twenty-five of whom it can be said:

To an architect he could talk as an architect; to an engineer, as an engineer; to a painter, as a painter; to a sculptor, as a sculptor; to a chemist, as a chemist; and so through all the branches of Engineering, Architecture, Art, and Science . . .[3]

My thanks are due to many people who helped in the preparation of this Exhibition, and detailed acknowledgements follow on page 178.

I acknowledge my profound thanks to Her Majesty the Queen for her gracious and most generous permission to use the Royal Archives and the Royal Library to research the Exhibition and this extended catalogue.

My gratitude is also due to national museums, public institutions and private owners in the United States, Germany, Eire and the United Kingdom for their generous help and the loan of many objects. This exhibition would not have been mounted without the efforts of many people, including H.R.H. the Duke of Gloucester, Nicholas Jenkins, the designer, and the many other members of the Advisory and Organizing Committees under the chairmanship of Reg Gadney of the Royal College of Art.

I should also like to thank the sponsors of the Exhibition, *The Observer* newspaper and The Midland Bank, for giving me an opportunity to work on the life and achievements of this remarkable man, and thus fulfil a long-cherished ambition.

HERMIONE HOBHOUSE London, 1983

Opposite
Prince Albert, by
Sebastian Ekkhardt.

CHAPTER ONE

'The Little Fellow
is the Pendant to the Pretty Cousin'

1 Prince Albert's mother: the Duchess Luise of Saxe-Coburg-Gotha, as a girl of sixteen. By Grassi.

Prince Albert was born at the Schloss Rosenau near Coburg, on August 26, 1819. His delighted grandmother, the Dowager Duchess of Saxe-Coburg-Saalfeld, wrote to her daughter, the Duchess of Kent, in London:

Louischen . . . was yesterday morning safely and quickly delivered of a little boy. Siebold, the accoucheuse, had only been called at three, and at six the little one gave his first cry in this world, and looked about like a little squirrel with a pair of large black eyes . . . I . . . found the little mother slightly exhausted, but gaie and dispos . . .

Louise is much more comfortable here than if she had been laid up in town. The quiet of this house, only interrupted by the murmuring of the water, is so agreeable. But I had many battles to fight to assist her in effecting her wish . . . No one considered the noise of the palace at Coburg, the shouts of children, and the rolling of the carriages in the streets . . .

She added that the child was to be called Albert, and that his godparents were to be herself, the Emperor of Austria, the Dukes of Gotha and of Saxe-Teschen, and the Count Emmanuel Mensdorff-Pouilly, who was married to her eldest daughter, Princess Sophie.[1]

Francis Charles Augustus Albert Emmanuel, Prince of Saxe-Coburg was the second son of Duke Ernest I (1784–1844) and his young wife Luise of Gotha (1800–1831). They had been married in 1817, when she was only 16. Her mother-in-law described her when she arrived in Coburg:

It is a charming, tiny being, not beautiful, but very pretty, through grace and vivacity. Every feature of her face has expression, her big blue eyes often look so sad from under her black lashes, and then again, she is a happy wild child . . . I hope she will still grow, as she is very short . . .[2]

It was a family tradition that Albert was very like his mother: an old servant who had known the Duchess Luise told Queen Victoria that, on seeing the grown-up Prince Albert for the first time in 1844, she had been overcome by the resemblance.[3]

The young Duchess's letters to her childhood friend Augusta von Studnitz reveal all the enjoyment of a high-spirited girl in the new grand life as a married lady in Coburg. 'Oh it is too beautiful. It is like being in paradise, and it is not wanting in an Angel.'[4] It was also bewildering. Her first son, Ernest, arrived in the following June, and the young mother wrote:

I wish my beloved Augusta could see the little child, it has big eyes, which are till now dark blue, but I am constantly hoping that they will become dark brown. The mouth is small and pretty and the face has a pretty shape . . . You cannot realise what a strange feeling I have being a respectable mamma. I love my little child very much, but I cannot believe that it is supposed to belong to me . . .[5]

At first it was all pleasure for the young Duchess. She could

accompany her 'beloved husband' to the chase, to hear the 'tender calling of the stags'. She could sit with him in the pretty garden of the Rosenau, could celebrate his birthday with a feast in the grand Riesensaal of the Schloss Ehrenburg. However, after the births of the two princes the couple drifted apart, the Duke to other amorous interests, which did not, however, prevent him scolding his young wife at the first hint of gossip.

If he had been sensible, he would have laughed also, but he took it seriously, and was angry with me. We talked about it and the whole ended in tears . . . Now he watches me, which he has never done before, and he misconstrues everything . . .[6]

This letter to Augusta was written in 1820. It was a difficult situation: the marriage between the teen-age girl and the sophisticated Duke, who had grown up in the dangerous world of Napoleon, and who had known both Vienna and Paris. In many ways he was a model ruler who granted a constitution to his people in 1821, and reorganized the finances of his Duchy, almost bankrupt on his accession. Duke Ernest I also had a fine collection of both French and Viennese furniture, and rebuilt the Ehrenburg Palace in the middle of Coburg, but none of this seems to have created a bond with his young wife. Her indiscretions became public knowledge; those of the Duke were already well known.

In 1824, a formal separation by which Luise was to leave Coburg was arranged, largely through the influence of Maximilian von Szymborski, the Duke's confidant. 'The Duke was friendly towards me. We came to an understanding and parted with tears, for life. I am more sorry for him than for myself.'[7] In

3 The Green Saloon at Burglasschlosse, Coburg, in 1832. By Heinrich Kruppel.

a spontaneous gesture of support for the young Duchess, which also expressed their dislike of Szymborski, the townspeople and peasants of Coburg attempted to arrest her departure. She had gone to the Rosenau on her way out of Coburg and they seized her carriage, and dragged it with her in it back to Coburg, where they forced their Duke and Duchess to appear together on the balcony of the Ehrenburg.

But, despite the calls for 'unity and peace again in the dynasty', no reconciliation took place, and Luise left Coburg and her children for good soon after. 'Leaving my children was the most painful thing of all . . . they have whooping cough and said "Mamma cries because she has got to go, now, when we are ill." The poor little lambs, God bless them.'[8]

After her divorce in 1826, she married the Freiherr Alexander von Hanstein, but only survived some five years. When she was dying, in August 1831, her stepmother, the widowed Duchess of Gotha, wrote to Duke Ernest:

The sad state of my poor Luise bows me to the earth. . . . The thought that her children had quite forgotten her distressed her very much. She wished to know whether they ever spoke of her. I answered that they were far too good to forget her; that they did not know of her sufferings as it would grieve the good children too much.[9]

It seems clear that the Duchess Luise was the scapegoat for a marital breakdown for which she was not wholly or even mostly responsible. Not only the partisanship of the people of Coburg, well aware of how the Ducal family living in the centre of the town was conducting itself, but also the memories cherished by

Prince Albert make this clear. Queen Victoria recorded for Colonel Grey in 1864, the Prince's attitude to his mother. 'The Prince never forgot her, and spoke with much tenderness and sorrow of his poor mother, and was deeply affected in reading, after his marriage, the accounts of her sad and painful illness.'[10] Princess Louise was called after his mother, and was said to resemble her.

Most ironically, the remains of poor Duchess Luise were brought back to Coburg to lie beside those of her first husband in the family mausoleum, though she had in fact asked to be buried on Von Hanstein's estates. On their last visit to Coburg in 1860, the Queen and the Prince visited the mausoleum to see 'Albert's own mother's sarcophagus'.

Only after her death did Duke Ernest remarry, again to a younger bride, to his sister's daughter, Marie of Wurtemberg (1799–1860). This meant that the young princes were without mother or stepmother throughout much of their childhood. Two doting grandmothers, one in Coburg and one at Gotha, did a good deal to care for the two little boys, but the real parent was in fact 'Rath' Florschutz.

This remarkable man, a councillor at Coburg, was appointed to look after the two princes in 1823 and only resigned his charge when they left Bonn University in 1838. He came to the Coburg princes after looking after their cousins, the young sons of the Graf von Mensdorff-Pouilly. He seems to have taken complete charge of the two little boys when they were only four and five years old respectively, and their maternal grandmother expressed concern that their nurse was to be sent away.

Florschutz outlived Prince Albert, and was one of those whom the widowed Queen asked for a memorandum to help the Prince's biographers.[11] In this he gives a very detailed account of the life led by the two young princes, mostly at the Rosenau, under his close supervision. From childhood they were never separated, sharing a room high under the steep roof of the little schloss. Prince Albert showed it to the Queen, when he took her to Coburg in 1845.

Before breakfast we went upstairs to where my dearest Albert and Ernest used to live. It is quite in the roof, with a tiny bedroom on either side, in one of which they both used to sleep with Florschutz their tutor. The view is beautiful, and the paper is still full of holes from their fencing; and the very same table on which they were dressed when they were little.[12]

The Rosenau was the children's home in the spring and summer; in the winter they moved back into the town palace, the Ehrenburg. After the Dukedom of Gotha, some miles away, passed to their father, part of the year was spent there, either in

4 Rath Florschutz, tutor to the Princes, in 1860.

5 The room occupied by Prince Ernest and Prince Albert as boys, at the Schloss Rosenau. From a watercolour by F. Rothbart in the possession of H.M. the Queen.

6 A collection of shells contributed by the Prince to the Naturmuseum in Coburg. Even after his marriage he continued to take an interest in the collection and help to build it up. The *Conus betulinus* in the centre came from the Moluccas, the *Conus textile* above it from Madagascar; the other shells came from the coasts of Britain – the *Volupopsis norvegicus* at the top right from Northumberland, while the two heavily encrusted *Buccinium undatum* below are labelled Bantry.

the great town palace or at Rheinhardtsbrunn, the country palace he built in 1827.

The Rosenau with its stepped gables and single staircase turret is a relatively modest country house, standing in a small formal garden, on a little hill overlooking its park. There are splendid open views in all directions, and even today it is very much in the country. Through the valley below runs a stream with a waterfall bordered by hay-meadows. There was a little Switzerei, or wooden farmhouse, where the milking cows were kept. The two boys had their own gardens, and also their fort, which Albert took his wife to see twenty years later.

. . . we walked by the rock again, where Albert made me taste the excellent water; and then we walked to the opposite side to see the little fortification which Albert and Ernest dug and made when they were children, and which has remained perfect. It is close to the little garden and the inn.[13]

It was not a secluded childhood, for the townspeople used the park on public holidays, Coburg being, as Colonel Grey reminded his readers, 'less exclusive than England'. In the same way, the boys had a number of local playfellows with whom they played the usual childish games, make-believe taking the form of re-enacting scenes from German history: *Wallenstein's Camp* was one such scene; in others the boys took it in turns to be Duke of Burgundy or the Emperor, and it is clear that it was not always the little princes who took the most important parts. Arthur Mensdorff, a rather older cousin, recalled many years later that Albert had refused to attack a 'fortress' held by the other side, from the rear, on the grounds that this would be 'most unbecoming in a Saxon Knight, who should always attack the enemy in front'.[14]

There were also agreeable visits to the theatre and opera in Coburg. The Prince had a liking for practical jokes, once filling an older cousin's pockets with soft cream cheese for her to find when she collected her cloak after the theatre; in return she placed a basket of live frogs under the 11-year-old Prince's bed. A more scientific escapade was the scattering of 'a number of small glass vessels about the size of a pea, filled with sulphuretted hydrogen which he threw about the floor of the pit and boxes of the Theatre to the great annoyance and discomfiture of the audience, at whose confusion he was greatly delighted'.[15] There were also amateur theatricals for which the young Prince Albert showed talent, developing in his later adolescent years a considerable reputation as a mimic.

Albert thoroughly understood the naïveté of the Coburg national character, and he had the art of turning people's peculiarities into a source of fun. He had a natural talent for imitation, and a great sense of the ludicrous, either in persons or in things; but he was never severe or ill-natured: the general kindness of his disposition preventing him from pushing a joke, however he might enjoy it, so as to hurt any one's feelings. Every man has, more or less, a ridiculous side, and to *quiz* this, in a friendly and good-humoured manner is after all the pleasantest description of humour. Albert possessed this rare gift in an eminent degree.[16]

'Rath' Florschutz took his duties extremely seriously, aware of the particular problems of the motherless boys. The two boys did everything together throughout their childhood. 'Brought up together they went hand-in-hand in all things, whether at work or play. Engaging in the same joys and the same sorrows, they were bound to each other by no common feelings of mutual love.'[17]

This isolation was increased by the fact that their father was not always at Coburg, though when he was at home they always

7 Prince Ernest and Prince Albert of Saxe-Coburg, in 1831. By Sebastian Eckhardt.

took breakfast with him. Throughout the long summer, this was usually eaten out of doors, in one of a number of agreeable country seats in and around Coburg. Sometimes it was in the Festung, the ancient ruined fortress above the town, to be restored by Ernest II, sometimes it was in the Hof garten, the public park lying below the fortress, perhaps at the Callenberg, Ernest I's favourite country house, or with the Dowager Duchess at Ketschendorf. The frustrated tutor complained of the time wasted from their studies in traipsing round Coburg to suit Duke Ernest's choice of al fresco breakfast place, but it must have made a pleasant break for the boys who rose soon after six to begin their studies.[18] It was an agreeable childhood, though a timetable drawn up by Prince Albert at the age of 14 indicates an arduous but varied programme of studies, including ancient and modern history, geography, reading, writing, German grammar and composition, Latin, French and English, religious instruction, music, drawing and riding. There were two periods dedicated to 'exercises in memory' which must have stood him in good stead when he came to prepare his English speeches which he initially learnt off by heart.[19] He also studied chemistry and mathematics but with tutors other than Florschutz.

Prince Albert was always very interested in natural history and animals. He and Prince Ernest made a collection of specimens, which in time became the foundation of the Naturmuseum in Coburg. Later they purchased items on their travels as well.

He was prepared for his confirmation at the same time as

Ernest, not only by Florschutz, but also by Dr. Jacobi. The Lutheran tradition was extremely important in Coburg, whose rulers had lost the hereditary succession to the Electorate through their adherence to the Reformed Faith in 1547. The connection with Luther himself was treasured and the room in the Festung, where he had sheltered from the wrath of the Emperor, is still shown to visitors. Prince Albert's religion was always coloured by his strict Lutheran upbringing, though his period at Bonn University which was open to both Catholics and Protestants made him personally tolerant. He maintained an interest in Luther throughout his life, starting a collection of books and manuscripts associated with Luther for Coburg in 1860. He contributed some 900 items to the Lutherbibliothek before his death.

The confirmation of the two Princes in April 1835 was a public event of some importance. It began with an hour-long public examination in the Riesensaal, before members of the Ducal family, including the Dowager Duchess of Gotha, the household, the ministry and a great number of people representing the town and villages of Coburg. The following day the Princes were confirmed in the chapel of the Ehrenburg, and that afternoon a special service was held in the Cathedral, the Moritzkirche, after a solemn procession through the streets of Coburg. Finally, a grand banquet was held in the Riesensaal.

This splendid occasion took place on Palm Sunday, 1835, when Prince Ernest was 16 and Prince Albert only 15. To celebrate it, a medal was struck showing the two Princes' heads. Duke Ernest I distributed rewards and marks of favour to the Princes' tutors and others who had taken part in their education. It was, however, the townspeople who presented Councillor Florschutz with a diamond ring, to mark their gratitude for the part he had played in the upbringing of the Hereditary Prince and his brother.

The Princes' step-grandmother from Gotha, the stepmother of the unhappy Duchess Luise, was present at the ceremony, but a dry little note in the Gothaitsche Zeitung, records that the Duchess of Coburg, their stepmother, 'could not venture on the journey from Gotha to Coburg at this inclement season. But her best wishes undoubtedly attend her sons . . .'[20]

Prince Albert was born a 'lucky Coburg', so nicknamed because of their considerable worldly success. The English civil servant, Charles Greville, using the phrase in January 1840, pointed out that this luck, or perhaps good management, did not make them popular.

The Ducal house of Saxe-Coburg was a cadet house of the house of Saxony, whose Elector, later King, of Saxony held court at Dresden. The junior, or Albertine branch, was Roman

8 Martin Luther: *Von der babylonischen Gefangenschaft der Kirche*, German translation by Thomas Murner, 1520, Augsburg. This is one of the volumes collected by the Prince Consort for the Lutherbibliothek in Coburg, founded by him in 1860. *Of the Church's Captivity in Babylon* was the second of Martin Luther's great works on reform to be published in 1520. Originally published in Latin, and thus given a hearing throughout Christendom, it brought about the final breach with the Papacy. This translation was published the same year.

9 Princess Charlotte of Wales, wife of Prince Leopold of Saxe-Coburg, about 1816. By George Dawe.

Catholic; while the senior, or Ernestine branch, had early distinguished itself as a patron of the Lutheran religion, offering Martin Luther protection in the difficult early years of the Reformation. Coburg itself is a relatively small Thuringian principality, lying between Bavaria, always a large Roman Catholic German state, and the small margravates and dukedoms lying between Bavaria and Prussia proper in Franconia and the Rhineland. In the nineteenth century it was united first with Saalfeld, and then, in 1826, by family arrangement with the Dukedom of Gotha, whose male line had died out with Prince Albert's mother's father.

In such small principalities there was always a tradition that the younger sons would have to seek their fortunes elsewhere. One of the best known of earlier generations of Coburger sons was Prince Friederich-Josias (1737–1815) who pursued a very successful career in the Austrian service.

The duchy was already in some financial difficulties, largely owing to the extravagance of his brother, Duke Ernest Friederich (1724–1800) and his wife Princess Sophie Antoinette of Brunswick-Wolfenbuttel. She was, in the words of her grandson, 'too great a person for a small dukedom; but she brought into the family energy and superior qualities, above the minute twaddle of these small establishments.'[21]

Fortunately for Coburg, the next Duchess, Augusta Caroline Sophia Reuss Ebersdorf (1757–1831), displayed great energy and character. Queen Victoria recalled her very distinctly as a 'most remarkable woman, with a powerful energetic, almost masculine mind, accompanied with great tenderness of heart and extreme love for nature'.[22] She produced seven children, all of whom married well, and whose alliances were to make Coburg the dominant strain in all the progressive royal families of Europe in the later nineteenth century. By great good fortune Catherine the Great, Empress of Russia, sent for her to bring her three daughters to St. Petersburg to provide a bride for the Grand Duke Constantine. Although the marriage was not happy, the family was guaranteed powerful Russian protection, against the invading French forces and against other intriguing German principalities. The younger brothers Leopold and Ferdinand were taken into the Russian army, Prince Leopold being the first German prince to join the liberating army which finally turned Napoleon out of Germany in the course of 1813. He was decorated on the field of battle after the surrender at Kulm on September 30, receiving Russian, Prussian and Austrian honours.

To his military honours, he added considerable experience of diplomatic negotiations, taking part in the Congress of Vienna, and visiting England in 1814 in the suite of the Allied Sovereigns, the Emperor of Russia and the King of Prussia. On this occasion

10 Baron Stockmar in 1859.

he met Princess Charlotte, only child of the Prince Regent and heir to the throne of England. At this time it was intended that she should marry a Dutch prince but, when this came to nothing, Prince Leopold continued to correspond with her and ultimately won her hand, with her father's reluctant approval. She married him in 1816, smiling, it is said, at the words, 'With all my worldly goods I thee endow', because of her husband's poverty.[23] In fact, the English parliament, anxious to use their approval of her to mark their disapproval of her father, voted the young Coburger the generous allowance of £50,000 a year, and the title of Prince Consort.

Always thorough, the Coburg family promoted a book describing the background of the house of Saxe-Coburg, by one Frederic Stoberl, so that the English should know about the new husband of the heir to the throne. George Dawe painted a pair of splendid portraits, and the English public basked briefly in the unusual pleasure of having a royal couple whom they could admire and like.

For Princess Charlotte, married life with Prince Leopold was certainly her happiest time. Much of this was spent at Claremont House, near Esher, bought for the young couple in 1816. It was, however, tragically brief. In November 1817, Leopold's mother wrote in her diary of the daughter-in-law she had never seen:

Charlotte is dead! Good God! I cannot realise the gigantic tragedy . . . Poor, poor Leopold! . . . She is dead, the beautiful, charming good woman, the hope of a large population over which she would have ruled and whose death ruins the whole life happiness of Leopold![24]

Prince Leopold was genuinely devoted to her and wrote many years later of 'the ruin of this happy home, and the destruction at one blow of every hope and happiness of Prince Leopold. He had never recovered the feeling of happiness which had blessed his short married life'.[25] He was given great support by Baron Christian Stockmar and it is from this time that his dependence on Stockmar as an ally and family adviser dates.

Christian Stockmar was a Coburger, trained as a doctor, who came to England as Prince Leopold's physician. He negotiated for Prince Leopold over both the thrones of Greece and of Belgium, and was present from time to time in the various Coburg households. Thus he accompanied Prince Albert on his Italian tour, and he was called in by the Duchess of Kent to advise on how to improve family relations at Kensington Palace. He confirmed Prince Leopold's view that Albert would make Victoria a good husband, he negotiated the marriage contract with Palmerston. After the marriage he made a practice of spending every winter in England, with the royal family; every spring he stole away to Coburg, with the minimum of fuss, refusing always any formal leave-taking, often to the distress of his royal hosts.

Charlotte's death was a disaster for more than Prince Leopold. With her had perished her stillborn child, the 'fruit, with which she would have blessed her country'. None of her numerous uncles and aunts had at the time a legitimate heir; the country was faced with the prospect of the now-childless Prince of Wales being succeeded by one of his unpopular middle-aged brothers, probably with the further threat of dynastic instability.

However, the royal uncles were well aware of the possibilities now opening before them. The Duke of Kent, the fourth son, revived an earlier approach to Prince Leopold's widowed sister, Victoire. Despite Princess Charlotte's own encouragement of his courtship, he had been rejected in October 1816, but the championship of his brother, the Prince Regent, who offered to arrange for the guardianship of Victoire's children, Prince Charles and Princess Feodora of Leiningen, turned the scales. With all the royal Dukes, a strong incentive was the hope that a dismayed parliament would supplement their incomes in return for their addressing themselves to the dynastic problem. The Duke of Kent was arranging to part from Mme Saint Laurent, his mistress with whom he had lived happily for 27 years. He was a model partner, considerate and solicitous even after they had officially parted and he had married Princess Victoire of Saxe-Coburg. 'We must never lose sight,' he wrote to an old friend who was to call on Mme Saint Laurent, 'that our unexpected separation arose from the imperative duty I owed to obey the call of my family and my Country to marry, and not from the least diminution in an attachment which had stood the test of twenty eight years and which, but for that circumstance, would unquestionably have kept up the connection, until it became the lot of one or other of us to be removed from the world.'[26]

The Duke of Kent and Princess Victoire were married in the Riesensaal in the Schloss Ehrenburg at Coburg, on May 29, 1818, according to the rites of the Lutheran church. Two months later, on July 13, they were married at Kew Palace according to the rites of the Church of England, in a joint ceremony with an elder brother, the Duke of Clarence, later William IV, who was marrying Adelaide of Saxe-Meiningen. William, already the father of a fine family of Fitzclarences, who survived to cluster round the throne of their legitimate cousin, Victoria, never produced a legitimate heir who survived for more than a year. Of the other brothers, Ernest, Duke of Cumberland, succeeded as King of Hanover, where the Salic Law remained, and therefore the young Princess Victoria was ineligible. The Duke of Cambridge married Princess Augusta and sired three children, one of whom married the Duke of Teck, and produced Princess Mary (1867–1953), later wife of George V of England.

Of this spate of royal marriages, the shortest-lasting was the

most significant for England.

The Duke of Kent brought his bride back to England in the spring of 1819, to a most ill-prepared suite at Kensington Palace, and there on May 24 she was delivered of a little princess. The Duke wrote to his mother-in-law at Coburg,

The little girl is truly a model of strength and beauty combined . . . the dear mother and child are doing marvellously well. It is absolutely impossible for me to do justice to the patience and sweetness with which she behaved . . . for you will easily believe that I did not leave her from the beginning to the end.[27]

The Duke and Duchess were model parents, the Duchess breast-feeding her new daughter, confessing that she was 'over anxious in a childish way with the little one, as if she were my first child'. The Duke was extremely solicitous, fussing over the details of nursery management, very proud of his new daughter, commending her to his friends with the words: 'Take care of her for she will be Queen of England.'

It was a difficult time for the royal family: for the Prince Regent, declining in health, with a wife he hated, the sight of his brothers with their newly acquired wives, producing children one after another with the intention of providing an heir to succeed him cannot have been easy. 1819 saw the birth of a still-born child to the Duke of Clarence, his Heir-Presumptive; a son in March to the Duke of Cambridge; the Princess Victoria on

May 24; and three days later a son to the Duke of Cumberland. The result was a good deal of deliberate prejudice. Inevitably the Prince Regent vented his frustration on the rest of the family. Thus the Princess Victoria was not allowed to take any of the traditional English royal names. Her father had planned for her to be Victoire Georgina Alexandrina Charlotte Augusta, but the Prince Regent would only allow Alexandrina (after the Emperor of Russia, a godfather) and Victoria (after her mother). Her uncle also insisted that the ceremony should be a private one, with no splendid display of uniform and orders. He let no opportunity pass for slighting the Kent family, an attitude which was to continue for much of the Princess's childhood.

The Duke of Kent's own position was not helped by his extravagance which very shortly made it difficult for him to continue to live in London. That winter he took a house at Sidmouth, in the interests of economy, and it was at Woolbrook Cottage, Sidmouth, that he died of a mismanaged cold on January 23, 1820.

Fortunately for the Duchess, her brother Leopold had been in England, staying in Berkshire, and he and the invaluable Stockmar had arrived before the Duke had died. It was Prince Leopold who dealt with the undertakers, who took the Duchess and the little Princess away from Sidmouth, who negotiated for permission for the Duchess to remain in the Duke's apartments at Kensington Palace. After the Duke of Kent's death Prince Leopold became a second father to Victoria, providing for her from the comfortable income granted to him for life as Princess Charlotte's husband. He advised his sister on how best to manage in her widowhood. This was particularly necessary in view of the behaviour of her brother-in-law, the Prince Regent, now George IV, who was bent on sending Victoire back to her German palace at Amorbach, seat of her first husband, the Prince of Leiningen. Prince Leopold's role was early made public by Lord Castlereagh, who declared in Parliament that no official vote was necessary for the widow and child of the Duke of Kent, since 'Prince Leopold with great liberality, had taken upon himself the charge of the support and education of the infant princess.'[28]

The difficulties of Princess Victoria's childhood are well known: both the ostracism and dislike of her royal uncles, and the regime devised by Sir John Conroy, the Comptroller of the Duchess of Kent's Household. Young Victoria was very closely confined to Kensington Palace, to the society of her mother and the Baroness Lehzen, her governess, with her contacts with her own contemporaries restricted to the company of Sir John Conroy's daughters.

The legacy of the 'Kensington system' was Victoria's depen-

12 Queen Victoria's father, the Duke of Kent and Strathearn. After Sir William Beechey.

13 William Lamb, 2nd Viscount Melbourne (1779–1848). Engraving after Hayter, 1836. He was Prime Minister at Queen Victoria's accession and remained in office till 1841; it became 'his province to educate, instruct and form' his young sovereign, in Greville's view, 'the most interesting mind and character in the world'.

dence on Lehzen, which was to cause such trouble in her early married life, and her antipathy to her mother, which only the diplomacy and strong family feelings of Prince Albert finally cured.

The effect of her isolated childhood, taken all in all, was not as damaging as it could have been: as the young Queen, she showed herself to be a woman of remarkable self-confidence, both charming and extrovert. She was also extremely fortunate in her first Prime Minister: as her biographer, Cecil Woodham-Smith has said:

It was a stroke of good fortune . . . that such a man as Melbourne should have been at hand to give her a second education and fill the gaps left by her years of isolation at Kensington. She adored him. His charm, his wit, his 'stores of knowledge', his constant kindness and patience, the entertainment of his company were irresistible, while his manner to the Queen, the discretion and purity of his conduct were admired, respected and liked by the whole Court.[29]

However, there were problems for her Ministers in the management of an unmarried Queen, particularly one who had 'come from the nursery to the throne'. The problems with her mother would not cease until she had an establishment of her own; she needed a private secretary but this was a tricky appointment. Lord Grey wrote to Stockmar: 'The best thing for the Princess would be to marry soon, and to marry a Prince of ability. He, as her bosom friend, would then be her most natural and safest private secretary. Assuming that the Queen will marry soon . . .'[30]

It is unlikely that even Stockmar and Leopold who had selected Prince Albert, despite his youth and relative inexperience, as the husband of the Queen, realized how excellently he would fill the part. Gradually, to the roles of lover, husband and father, he would add those of political mentor and private secretary, so that she came to rely on him completely, 'giving up over twenty years, every year more, the habit of ever deciding anything on her own judgement . . .'[31]

Prince Albert said in later life that he had known since he was three that it was intended that he should marry his English cousin. This was the favourite scheme of their common grandmother, the Dowager Duchess Augusta. In 1821, she wrote to the Duchess of Kent: 'The little fellow is the pendant to the pretty cousin; very handsome, but too slight for a boy; lively, very funny, all good nature and full of mischief.'[32]

The plan had the support of Uncle Leopold, one of the most astute diplomatists in Europe. He was largely resident in England during the 1820s until he ascended the throne of Belgium in 1831, and his residence, Claremont, was one of Princess Victoria's childhood homes. He also visited Coburg frequently, and his visits were always a source of delight to his nephews. However, there is evidence that he and Stockmar, though clearly prejudiced in favour of a Coburg husband for the young Queen of England, were critical of the young Prince Albert and would not have approved his suit willy-nilly.

The cousins had first met in 1836, when Duke Ernest brought his two sons to England for a visit. Despite the opposition of William IV, who asked the Prince of Orange from the Netherlands to make a visit at the same time with his two sons, the visit went well. There was entertainment, a grand ball at Kensington Palace for the young people, a visit to the opera, a formal levee and dinner. The Princess seems to have expressed a preference for Ernest at this time and, whether this was serious or not, it was obvious to interested observers that Albert was not much of a courtier, and less interested in dancing and entertainment than the Princess, his cousin. He suffered, as contemporary biographers were at pains to point out, from being a 'lark', always more active in the early mornings, and subject to uncontrollable sleepiness during late evenings.

The Princess, however, wrote to King Leopold:

. . . I must thank you for the prospect of great happiness . . . in the person of Dear Albert. Allow me, my dearest Uncle, to tell you how delighted I am with him, and much I like him in any way. He possesses every quality that could be desired to make me perfectly happy. He is so sensible, so kind and so good and so amiable too. He had beside the most pleasing exterior and appearance that you could wish to see . . .[33]

More drily Albert recalled that they 'were much pleased with each other, but not a word in allusion to the future . . . passed between us . . .'[34] The Princess felt clearly that she had not committed herself for in July 1839 she was writing to Uncle Leopold, '. . . I may not have the feeling for him which is requisite to ensure happiness. I may like him as a friend, and as a cousin and a brother . . .'[35]

Meanwhile Albert and his brother had moved to Brussels, with Florschutz, and under the tutelage of a retired German officer who had served in the English German Legion. They studied with other tutors, including the famous statistician, M. Quetelet. They were lodged, not as part of King Leopold's household, but in a 'small but very pretty house with a little garden in front . . . and perfectly shut from the noise of the streets'.[36] Albert attended Belgian army manoeuvres under the aegis of King Leopold, staying in a 'very nice little hut, close to the Royal one, over which the Belgian and Saxon flags were hoisted'.[37] It is tempting to see in this excursion the seeds of the idea for the Aldershot field day and the Royal Pavilion which he promoted for the British. The

14 Page from Prince Albert's sketchbook in the Royal Library, Windsor Castle. This has a number of most interesting pages, many of which relate to military history and uniforms; some, like this one, give an entertaining view of life in 19th-century Coburg.

princes also visited the battlefield of Waterloo with Colonel von Weichmann who had himself fought there.

In April 1837 they moved to Bonn University, then one of the few universities to take both Protestant and Roman Catholic students. Here they lived in a house rented for them. There was a group of German princes at Bonn. Prince Albert was remembered as an assiduous student who 'liked above all things to discuss questions of public law and metaphysics, and constantly, during our many walks, juridical principles or philosophical doctrines were discussed . . .' He was also a more than competent fencer, winning at least one prize, and took part in student singsongs and amateur theatricals where he was a moving spirit. His talent for caricature and mimicry came into play at the expense of the learned professors.

The princes stayed at Bonn until August 1838, but their residence was interrupted by a lengthy tour to Northern Italy, then largely under the control of Austria, to Switzerland and the Tyrol and then briefly to Coburg, and the beloved Rosenau. It included a visit to Munich where Ludwig I was embarking on a programme of improvements, including the work to the Residenz where the Nazarenes were decorating the Hall of the Niebelungen, in a manner which was to inspire the fresco painting in the House of Lords some ten years later.

It was now time for the two princes to follow their separate careers: Ernest was to go to Dresden to train in the Saxon army, 'to sacrifice himself to Mars', Albert to Italy. The latter found the parting from Ernest, coming on top of the breakup of the little group at Bonn, almost unsupportable. Even so, he was concerned over his brother's feelings: 'I shall not set out,' he wrote to his friend, William von Lowenstein, 'till Ernest also launches his vessel, so that he may not be left behind alone. The separation will be frightfully painful to us. Up to this moment, we have never . . . been a single day away from each other.'[38]

Prince Albert set out with his father as far as Munich, and then on his Italian tour proper, travelling this time with Baron Stockmar and an English officer who had been selected by King Leopold as a travelling companion, and who had been seconded from the British army for the purpose. Lieutenant Francis Seymour (1813–1890), who was later appointed to his suite, recalled the Prince as being 'slight in figure and rather tall, his face singularly handsome and intelligent, his features regular and delicate; his complexion, which, later, from exposure to an Italian sun became brown, was then fair and clear. He had . . . a great look of goodness and distinction . . .'[39]

Albert spent January and February in Florence, studying Italian, reading English with Seymour, working at his music, composing, singing and playing the piano and the organ. He visited artists' studios as well as galleries, but Seymour emphasises his love of country walks, something which stayed with him through life. He left Florence on March 12 for Naples and Rome, which he found disappointing. Again he visited the studios of living artists as well as galleries, including that of Hugo Wolff, whose statue of him was to adorn the staircase at Osborne. He attended the Easter week celebrations in St. Peter's Square. He had the honour of an audience with the Pope, with whom he appears to have discussed Greek art, the 'old gentleman' maintaining that they were influenced by the Etruscans, his young visitor contending, in spite of Papal infallibility, that it was the Egyptians who had the greater influence.

Prince Albert was concerned at this critical time by a delay proposed by the Queen, not so much because she objected to her cousin, but because she wished to put off getting married for four years. He had conceived the 'quiet but firm resolution to declare, that I also tired of the delay withdrew from the affair'.[40] He was concerned that if he waited for four years and was then rejected his matrimonial prospects, indeed his whole prospects for life would be hopelessly prejudiced.

It was therefore with no great feelings of optimism that he set out with Prince Ernest for England in October 1839.

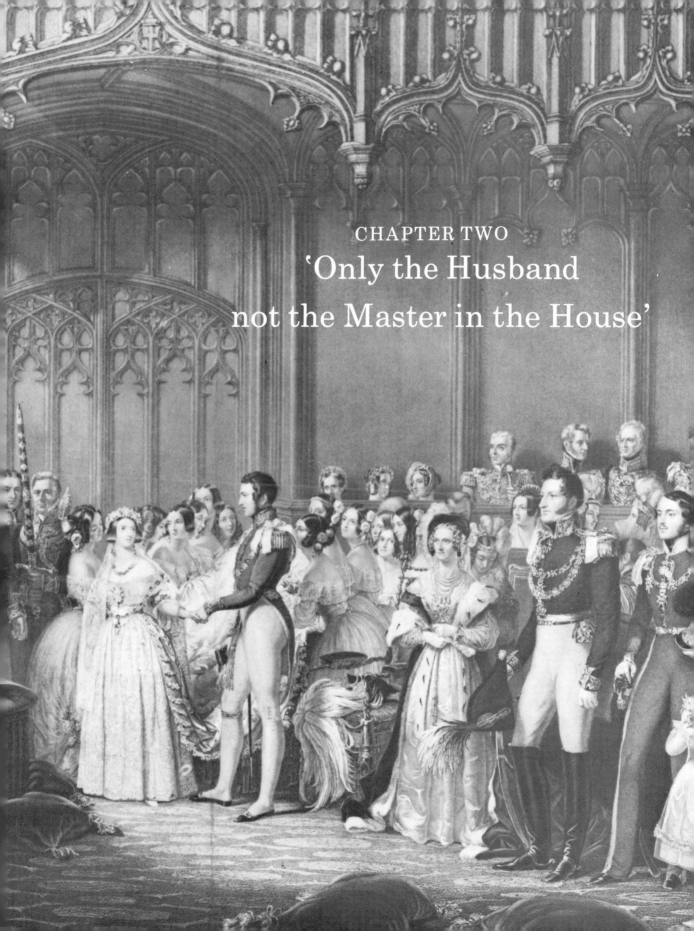

CHAPTER TWO

'Only the Husband
not the Master in the House'

The Princes arrived in England on October 10, 1839, reaching Windsor Castle just before dinner, which they were unable to attend because their baggage with their evening clothes had gone astray. However, they joined the other guests after dinner, in spite of still being in morning dress.[1] For the next few days, they remained at Windsor Castle, joining in the Queen's regular routine. This included a morning visit to the Queen who breakfasted alone, family luncheon with the Queen and 'Aunt Kent', and then riding in the afternoon, the cavalcade usually including the Prime Minister and other Ministers in attendance.

The Queen made up her mind quickly: there would be no waiting for three or four years. She sent for Prince Albert on October 15. 'I said to him,' she recorded in her *Journal*,

that I thought he must be aware *why* I wished him to come here, and that it would make me *too happy* if he would consent to what I wished (to marry me); we embraced each other over and over again, and he was *so* kind, *so* affectionate; Oh! to *feel* I was, and am, loved by *such* an Angel as Albert was *too great a delight to* describe! he is *perfection*; perfection in every way — in beauty — in everything! I told him I was quite unworthy of him . . . he said he would be very happy . . . and was so kind and seemed so happy, that I felt it was the happiest brightest moment in my life, which made up for all I had suffered and endured.

With considerable perspicacity and consideration, she added '. . . I will strive to make him feel as little as possible the great sacrifice he has made; I told him it was a great sacrifice — which he wouldn't allow . . .'[2]

Despite his chivalrous disclaimer, and the fact that the Prince had been groomed from his early years for the role of Queen Victoria's husband, he realized that his new position would entail sacrifices. He was always insistent to his relations that he would be 'untiring in my efforts and labours for the country to which I shall in future belong, and where I am called to so high a position'.[3] Writing to his stepmother, his outlook seems almost too pessimistic:

With the exception of my relations towards [the Queen] my future position will have its dark sides, and the sky will not always be blue and unclouded. But life has its thorns in every position, and the consciousness of having used one's powers and endeavours for an object so great as that of having promoted the good of so many, will surely be sufficient to support me . . .[4]

The first 'thorn' would be the exile from his beloved Coburg and Gotha, and from the closely knit, though far-flung, family circle with whom he had grown up, and from contemporaries like William von Lowenstein. He wrote optimistically to his grandmother of 'running over occasionally' to see all his dear relations, and assured her he would always remain 'a true German, a true Coburger'. In fact, though the Queen travelled more widely than any previous English sovereign, for reasons of State

Previous page
15 The marriage of Queen Victoria and Prince Albert in the Chapel Royal, St. James's Palace, February 10, 1840. Engraved by C. E. Wagstaff, after Sir George Hayter.

16 Lithograph of Prince Albert and Queen Victoria, printed and distributed in Coburg and Berlin.

VICTORIA.

ALBERT.

they could not often go to Coburg, and she always resented the Prince's absences, even on official business, which were therefore kept to a minimum. They only made two visits together to Coburg during his lifetime and, though he sometimes went by himself, these were fleeting visits connected with family business.

Prince Albert returned to Coburg to make his adieux on November 14, and the Queen made her announcement to her Privy Council on November 23. Greville, the Clerk to the Council, an astringent recorder of the great events of the period wrote:

> . . . The Queen came in, attired in a plain morning gown, but wearing a bracelet containing Prince Albert's picture. She read the declaration in a clear sonorous, sweet-toned voice but her hands trembled so excessively that I wonder She was able to read the paper which she held . . .[5]

The royal family had been told previously, the Duchess about three weeks after the proposal, something she bitterly resented. The public announcement was now made. Reactions were mixed: there were accusations of fortune-hunting, irritation that the 'lucky Coburgs' had married on to yet another throne, some cartoons which recorded the English dislike of both Germans and Coburgers,

> . . . One her German Cousin brought, I mean a plain gold ring,
> Our pretty Queen's accepted it, and that without a frown,
> And just by way of recompense, she gave him *half a crown*.[6]

There was of course, the usual public rejoicing which accom-

panies the wedding of an attractive royal couple. There were sentimental ballad sheets, portraits of the young Queen and her Prince, and only the occasional sour reminder that:

> . . . He comes to take, 'for better or for worse',
> England's fat Queen and England's fatter purse.[7]

The Times waited till the wedding day itself to observe:

. . . If the thing were not finally settled indeed, one might, without being unreasonable, express a wish that the consort selected for a Princess so educated and hitherto so unfairly guided, as Queen Victoria, should have been a person of riper years, and likely to form more sound and circumspect opinions . . .[8]

However, the way in which this 'youth' dealt with the immediate problem which faced him on his accession show him to have been circumspect beyond his years. It was also fortunate, perhaps, that he was still a relatively pliable and amenable character because he might otherwise have rebelled against some of the circumstances of his early married life. Leopold's letter to Melbourne reveals his concern and affection.

'The position of a husband of a Queen, who reigns in her own right, is a position of the greatest difficulty for *any person* and at *any time* . . . Albert, altho' young, is steady very much beyond his years, has very good sense and an equally good judgement. He is pure minded and well behaved, has a decided turn for scientific occupations and from a natural gay, candid and amiable disposition, he seems very little inclined to forget himself and to meddle with affairs . . . of which he understand nothing . . . But the success *we all desire* will depend on the good sense and right *not of one alone* . . . It is my most intimate conviction, that a really sensible husband may be the most *useful* the *safest* and the *best friend a sovereign Queen can have*'. King Leopold went on to remind Melbourne of the importance of the young Queen's approach . . . 'as *the only man*, who can fully speak out to her, and by doing so, establish *in time* in *her young mind*, a proper and correct view of . . . *the high importance of the union she is about to form.*'[9]

Other questions were matter for public debate, and here the ineptness of the government's handling of the marriage question and the Queen's 'hatred of everything Tory' did him great disservice. First was the question of his annuity as the Queen's husband, and in this matter the House of Commons remembered only too well the famous case of his uncle who had enjoyed his annuity for over a decade after the death of Princess Charlotte. The usual figure granted to royal consorts was £50,000 and this was proposed by Lord John Russell but without prior consultation with the Opposition. In the event, it was reduced to £30,000 on a motion by a Tory member, Colonel Sibthorp, who was later to oppose the Prince again over the Crystal Palace. Many Whigs and Radicals supported the motion because of the poor state of the economy, and the Queen and the Prince had to accept the lower figure, the Prince observing that this would necessarily reduce his patronage of the arts.[10]

The question of his precedence proved insuperable largely because of the attitude of the House of Hanover. Characteristically, it was the Queen's uncle, the King of Hanover, who proved most difficult, but the old Duke of Wellington led the opposition in the House of Lords where the matter was raised as part of a bill naturalizing the Prince. In the event the attempt to grant the Prince precedence by Act of Parliament was dropped, and he was given 'place preeminence, and precedence next to Her Majesty', by Royal Letters Patent.

This solved the problem in England but, as the Queen herself observed, 'abroad, the Prince's position was always a subject of negotiation and vexation: the position accorded to him the Queen always had to acknowledge as a favour bestowed on her . . .'

Albert had refused an English title against the advice of King Leopold, so he remained Prince of Saxe-Coburg and Gotha. The Queen raised the question of giving him the title of King Consort on several occasions but only in 1857 was he officially given the title of Prince Consort, again by Royal Letters Patent.[11] He was given the right to quarter the Royal Arms by Royal Warrant, marshalling the Royal Arms of England in the most important place, placing the arms of Saxony in the inferior quarters where those of a wife would normally be put.

18 The Arms of the Prince Consort.

Opposite, top
19 *The Wonder of Windsor*. A satirical lithograph of 1841, by Charles Hunt, showing the Coburg family. Prince Albert on the left, seated at a desk; his uncle, King Leopold of the Belgians, playing the violin in the centre; his cousin, King Ferdinand of Portugal, behind at the window; his brother, Ernest, at the piano; his aunt, the Duchess of Kent, in the doorway behind the Queen.

Opposite, bottom
20 Prince Albert on the road from Dover in February, 1840, escorted by a Guard of Honour of the 11th Light Dragoons, later the 11th Hussars. Lithograph by G. F. Bragg.

The Prince had returned to Germany in November, and in January two members of his suite, Viscount Torrington and Colonel Grey, arrived in Coburg to invest him with the Garter and to accompany him to England. After calling on King Leopold in Brussels, the royal party embarked on the *Ariel* at Calais, arriving seasick and prostrate at Dover on February 6.

The wedding took place on Monday, February 10, 1840, in the chapel of St. James's Palace, and the honeymoon was spent at Windsor.

A large crowd cheered the royal couple in St. James's Park, and on the way to Windsor. There were criticisms of the Queen's behaviour, partly over her favouritism to the Whigs in her invitations, where, in Greville's words, she 'had been wilful, obstinate, and wrongheaded as usual'. The briefness of the honeymoon also caused talk: Lady Palmerston criticized the Queen's indelicacy in sending for an immense party to join them on the Wednesday, and holding an impromptu dance at Windsor Castle on the Thursday. Greville found the couple's style 'poor and

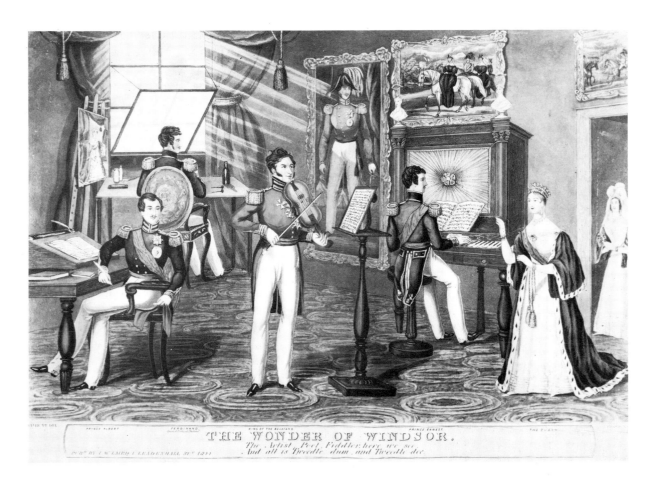

THE WONDER OF WINDSOR.
The Artist, Poet, Fiddler; here we see
And all is Tweedle dum, and Tweedle dee.

21 Earthenware plate celebrating the wedding of Queen Victoria. One of a number of popular ceramic pieces commemorating the occasion.

shabby', with the postillions in undress uniform and 'no new chariot', while he was shocked at the bridal couple's early rising, and told Lady Palmerston that 'this was not the way to provide us with a Prince of Wales'.[12]

Prince Albert early discovered that there were problems in being the husband of a Queen regnant, largely because his position was little understood in England. However, despite the traditional dislike of foreigners, he found himself a series of roles, first as the Queen's consort, and then increasingly in his own right. The role of 'mari de Madame' is more often a source of humour than of admiration, but Prince Albert is one of the few men who have made it a successful career. Nonetheless, even he found his position uneasy at first, complaining with great frankness to William von Lowenstein: 'I am very happy and contented; but the difficulty in filling my place with the proper dignity is that I am only the husband, not the master in the house.'[13]

By perseverance, hard work, and a modest but determined effort to have things about him ordered to his liking, he gradually created for himself a position in national life, ultimately earning the respect of the aristocratic clique who ran the country. In the early years of their married life the Queen deliberately excluded him from any official business, against the explicit advice of Melbourne. As she confessed to him when he praised the Prince's reception on an official occasion, 'I don't like it – first because I don't like his being absent from me, and then because I dislike his taking my part in politics or in the general affairs of the country.'[14]

The frustrations of being excluded from his wife's preoccupations with affairs of state was increased by the situation in the royal Household. The Queen had already had her Household, into which he moved, and one of the most influential figures was the Baroness Lehzen, the Queen's former governess. Lehzen had been an indispensable ally during the Queen's difficult adolescence, and had reaped her reward at the Queen's accession, having virtual control of the Queen's private expenditure. This meant that she controlled much of what went on both at Windsor and Buckingham Palace, with considerable success, being 'much beloved by the women and much liked and esteemed by all who frequent the Court'. She would not acknowledge that the Prince now had authority in the Household, complaining that 'he had slighted her in the most marked manner and she was too proud not to resent it'. The Queen's biographer, Cecil Woodham-Smith, has suggested that the Queen was almost frightened of Lehzen, and that the continual tension in the household was bad for her nerves. Ultimately, after two years of married life the Prince had acquired enough influence to be able to despatch Lehzen with dignity to Germany for a holiday for her health, never to return.[15]

The Prince's influence was very much strengthened by the

22 *Tender Annuals*, cartoon commenting on the regularity and number of the births of the royal children. By W. Kohler, c. 1843. 'Hollo! Hollo! Young fellow, come, come, I shall have such a *stock* of them *sort* o'plants on my hands I sha'nt know what to do with them.'

23 *Albert and Victoria*, engraving by Prince Albert after Queen Victoria, showing the Prince of Wales and the Princess Royal in the nursery. The Queen and Prince Albert were both enthusiastic amateur artists.

arrival of their first child. The Queen's pregnancy increased her popularity: the whole country was only too aware of the parallel with the unfortunate Princess Charlotte. However, all went well: the Princess Royal arrived on November 22 and the Queen made a rapid recovery under the tender care of the Prince, who always nursed her with great devotion throughout her numerous pregnancies. 'No one but himself ever lifted her from her bed to her sofa . . . For this purpose he would come instantly when sent for . . . As years went on and he became overwhelmed with work this was often done at much inconvenience to himself.'[16]

The Queen and the Prince were disappointed that it was not

24 Prince Albert and the Prince of Wales with Baron Stockmar and other members of the Household. From left to right: Sir Charles Phipps, Mr. Gibbs, Albert Edward, Prince of Wales, Prince Albert, Baron Stockmar, Dr. Becker, Baron Ernst Stockmar.

a son, though the Prince came to lavish all a father's devotion on his intelligent, able, eldest daughter, Vicky. In fact the Queen discovered to her dismay that she was pregnant again early the next year, and the Prince of Wales arrived on November 9.

Public enthusiasm for the royal family was slightly diminished thereafter by the regular arrival of royal babies and, by 1843, this became a subject for cartoonists. The Prince was seen as an all too successful nurseryman propagator, while *Punch* forecast that by 1860 there would be a 'Royal Lady that lived in a shoe . . .'[17] Fortunately for both the country's loyalty and the Queen, who had her reservations about being the mother of a large family, the 'tender annuals' became less frequent. But the royal family was large, and it was a tribute to the royal nursery that all the babies survived to marry and provide the Queen with grandchildren. Much of this was due to the Prince who took an enlightened interest in the way the nursery was managed, and who provided his children with a healthy home life in the many royal homes which he built and improved.

Much has been written on the childhood of the royal children, particularly that of the Prince of Wales, whose upbringing was apparently the least successful. However, Sir Philip Magnus, in his biography of Edward VII, makes the point that the Prince, unlike the Queen, 'tried to treat his children as equals; and they were able to penetrate his stiffness and reserve because they realised instinctively not only that he loved them but that he enjoyed and needed their company.' It is interesting to follow Magnus in the contrasting of the Prince's need of his children with the Queen's confession that she was not particularly interested in the company even of the older children (this was in 1856) because of her own solitary childhood.[18]

Lady Lyttelton, who was governess to the royal children, records many anecdotes of the Prince's kindness and patience with the children.[19] His entertainments for his children provided the subjects for a number of broadsheets, and humorous illustrations. At Osborne he tried to provide something of the life he and Ernest had enjoyed at Rosenau, giving the children gardens, a fort, even a Swiss cottage, a gigantic dolls' house where they could play at shops and housekeeping.

25 *The Queen and Prince Albert at Home.*

THE QUEEN AND PRINCE ALBERT AT HOME.

26 Christmas trees at Windsor, showing the small trees for the Duchess of Kent and the Royal children, in 1850. From a watercolour painted for the Royal Collection by John Roberts.

27 The Prince Consort's Birthday Table, August 26, 1859. The gifts included a stuffed deer, now in the Museum at Osborne, and the stork ceramic fountain, now in the Dairy at Frogmore, then under construction.

Opposite, top left
29 Prince Albert as Edward III.

Opposite, top middle
30 Music sheet for the Court Ball held on June 6, 1845, when guests wore costumes of the reign of George II. Specially composed and arranged music was often published for grand occasions.

Opposite, top right
31 Portrait of Prince Ernest and Prince Albert in medieval costume by Maguire. There was a fine collection of armour at Coburg.

Christmas was always spent at Windsor, and this was the favourite festival of the Prince: 'a day, for the interchange of presents, as marks of mutual affection and good will. Christmas trees were set up in the Queen's and Prince's rooms, and in another room for the young Princes and Princesses, and in the oak-room for the household.'[20] The presents were distributed on Christmas Eve. He instituted this practice on the first Christmas of their married life. His example undoubtedly popularized the Christmas tree in England, but it had already been imported by Queen Charlotte, who as a Princess had known Christmas trees in her native Germany.

Court balls were an important part, not only of court life but also of the social and political scene. The Queen irritated Lord

PRINCE ALBERT AS EDWARD III.

THE COURT BALL MARCH
AND
THE MINUET D'EXAUDET

HER MAJESTY'S BAL COSTUMÉ
27 JUNE 1842

JULLIEN,

Above
28 The performance of *Macbeth* in the Rubens Room, Windsor Castle, on February 4, 1853. Painted by Louis Haghe for the Queen.

John Russell, when Prime Minister, by insisting on holding her balls on Friday, which was a day set aside in the House of Commons for government business. Equally some of the grandest of the balls had political overtones – the famous *Bal Costumé* of May 1842 had a mediaeval theme, and the Queen and the Prince went as Queen Philippa and Edward III. Scholarly research went into the design of the costumes, both of the royal couple and their guests, and these were recorded in a book and in a magnificent portrait by Landseer. Both this ball, and one held at Covent Garden Theatre a fortnight later had the noble intention of helping the Spitalfield weavers. In 1848, the Queen incurred the wrath of the government by decreeing that

EDWARD OXFORD FIRING AT THE QUEEN AND PRINCE ALBERT ON
CONSTITUTION HILL, JUNE 10th 1840.

Published by the Proprietor, 5, Little S? Thomas Apostle & may be had at 63, Fetter Lane.

32 Contemporary card showing the attempted assassination of the Queen in June 1840. Oxford fired twice but missed, and the Royal couple then continued to the Duchess of Kent's house in Belgrave Suare. 'From thence we took a short drive through the park, partly to give Victoria a little air, and partly to show the public we had not lost all confidence in them.' The popularity of both the Queen and the Prince was much increased by the incident.

everyone should wear British-made clothes at her drawing-rooms.[21]

In 1845, the Duke and Duchess of Nemours, of the French royal family, were entertained to a fancy dress party based on the court of George II, '. . . all the elderly folk of both sexes dressing themselves up and learning to dance minuets'.[22]

Entertainments at Windsor included theatricals, both amateur and professional. Charles Keen was appointed Director of the Windsor Theatricals, a post he held from 1848 until 1859. Dramatic entertainments were encouraged for the children, including tableaux with a topical flavour.

Both the Queen and the Prince liked riding, and the Prince enjoyed hunting and shooting because of the opportunity to be in the open air. English public opinion was very selective: they applauded the Prince for following the Belvoir Hunt in 1843, at a meet at Harlaxton, on a day when even Anson fell off. The Queen could write to Uncle Leopold: '. . . Albert's riding so well and so boldly and so hard has made such a sensation that it has been written all over the country . . . it has put an end to all sneering for the future about Albert's riding.'[23]

CHAPTER THREE

The Queen's Secretary

34 George Edward Anson (1812–49), the Prince's secretary during his first years in England. Lithograph by T. Fairland after George Richmond. Anson died very suddenly, leaving the 'Prince and the Queen in floods of tears and quite shut up. It is to them a heavy loss indeed, irreparable – I mean that so warm a *friend* they can hardly expect to find again, in ever so trustworthy and efficient a servant and minister.' (Lady Lyttelton.)

Previous page
33 Oil sketch for a portrait of the Prince, by Sir Francis Grant. Design for a grand portrait commissioned by Christ's Hospital, after a Royal visit in 1846, which now hangs in the hall of Christ's Hospital in Horsham.

Prince Albert discovered that there were even greater problems in finding a constitutional place than a domestic one. Many years later he complained to Stockmar:

A very considerable section of the nation had never given itself the trouble to consider what really is the position of the husband of a Queen Regnant. When I first came over here, I was met by this want of knowledge and unwillingness to give a thought to the position of this luckless personage. Peel cut down my income, Wellington refused me my rank, the Royal Family cried out against the foreign interloper, the Whigs in office were only inclined to concede to me just as much space as I could stand on. The Constitution is silent as to the Consort of the Queen . . .[1]

In fact, the Prince carved himself a very important place, if not in the constitution at least in the government of the country, so much so that on his death Florence Nightingale observed, 'He was really a minister. This very few knew. He neither liked nor was liked, but what he has done for this country no one knows.'[2]

One of the first problems with which he was confronted was that of appointing a Household, a group of noblemen and gentlemen, who would be acceptable to him personally, but also able to deal with his official and ceremonial duties. At that time the ladies and gentlemen of the Royal Household were overtly political appointments, and were 'changed' when a government of a different political complexion came into office. Only in the course of Queen Victoria's reign did the distinction between political and non-political appointments to the Household become established. In May 1839, the Queen had checkmated a proposal that Sir Robert Peel should form a government on the grounds that he had wished to 'dismiss her ladies' and change some of them for Tory adherents.

Less partisan than the Queen, more perspicacious in his approach than Lord Melbourne, the Prince argued for a Household above party:

. . . the selection should be made without regard to politics; for if I am really to keep myself free from all parties, my people must not belong exclusively to one side. Above all, the appointments should not be mere 'party rewards', but they should possess other recommendations . . . Let them be either of very high rank, or very rich, or very clever, or persons who have performed important services for England . . . above all I do wish that they should be well-educated men and of high character, who shall have already distinguished themselves in their several positions, whether it be in the army, or navy, or in the scientific world.[3]

Despite this definite expression of neutrality expressed in a letter to the Queen on December 10, he was firmly given George Anson, formerly secretary to Lord Melbourne himself, as his private secretary. In the event he became very fond of Anson, and the appointment was a great success.

He was very outspoken in his desire that his Household should

35 General the Hon. Charles Grey (1804–70), who became the Prince's secretary after Anson's death, later serving as Queen Victoria's private secretary. He was the son of Earl Grey, of the Reform Bill, and the brother of the Whig politician who was interested in Army reform, the 3rd Earl Grey. Photograph taken in 1860.

be non-partisan, and suggested to Melbourne that 'the establishment is formed according to *my* views and then I have a mixed household of whigs and tories, who remain with me during *every* administration in order to prove thereby to the nation that *I will belong to no party*.' He set out his views on the great English political parties to Uncle Leopold soon after his marriage: 'I do not think it necessary to belong to any party. Composed as party is here of two extremes both must be wrong. The Whigs seek to change *before change* is required. The love of change is their great fling. The Tories on the other hand *resist change* long after the feeling and the temper of the times has loudly demanded it . . . My endeavour will be to form my opinions quite apart from politics and party, and I believe that such an attempt may succeed . . .'[4]

In the course of time, he was able to choose his own Household, and establish the idea of a sovereign and throne above party. He was unorthodox, however, in some of his appointments, choosing men unacceptable to his more aristocratic gentlemen. Charles Phipps wrote to him many years later, opposing the appointment of the scientist Lyon Playfair:

'. . . The qualities of Dr. Playfair are those of a learned Chemist, a Geologist, and a public Lecturer – none of these appear to me to be the attributes that render a man fit to be a Gentleman Usher to Your Royal Highness. Dr. Playfair is a man of low birth, ordinary appearance and uncouth manners, all these are disqualifications . . . appointments about the Court could be made the means of distinguishing high talent and scientific attainment, but in my humble opinion these qualifications should be combined with the other necessary qualities of birth or position . . . A Court,' he reminded the Prince, 'is necessarily aristocratic.[5]

In addition to the more official appointments the Prince brought with him the Baron Stockmar, a peripatetic member of the royal Household until 1857, and a number of persons to fill humbler appointments. These included his German librarians, Dr. Emil Edward Praetorius, who retired in 1846 and was succeeded by Herr Carl Friedrich Meyer,[6] and Dr. E. Becker, an early photographer. He made other German appointments, his Stallmeister, or Gentleman Rider, who apparently supervised his horses, was Herr William Meyer, and his valet Cart, who had looked after the Princes when they were children, was Swiss.[7]

The Prince consolidated his position by undertaking the role of the sovereign's secretary.

This was an informal post which had existed under George III and his sons. It was a very sensitive appointment; and, when Queen Victoria had come to the throne 'fresh from the nursery', Lord Melbourne had taken upon himself this time-consuming task which, of course, involved not only helping the young

Left
36 Lord John Russell (1792–1878), later
Earl Russell, a distinguished Whig
politician, and Prime Minister from 1846 to
1852. He belonged to the coterie of Whigs
who surrounded the Queen on her
accession, but irritated her and the Prince
by his inability to control Palmerston,
Foreign Secretary in his Cabinet.

Middle
37 The 14th Earl of Derby (1799–1869).
Prime Minister twice – in 1852 and again
in 1858.

Right
38 3rd Viscount Palmerston (1784–1865),
nicknamed Pilgerstein by the Queen and the
Prince, and notoriously unpopular with
them for his aggressive and independent
conduct of foreign policy, which often
caused embarrassment with foreign
sovereigns. He became Prime Minister in
1855, a post which he held with one
intermission until his death, in 1865.

All three photographs are from a collection
of *cartes de visites* in the Royal Archives, of
1860.

Queen deal with her official correspondence but giving her training in a number of constitutional and governmental matters
which her isolated and secluded education had omitted. He fore-
saw that this position could not continue, not least because, with
a change of government, the Queen would lose not only her
Prime Minister but her own office and secretary for dealing with
public business. Her marriage was seen as a solution to the
problem, and it was hoped from the first that her husband would
fill this role.

Queen Victoria did not show any great enthusiasm for con-
sulting her new husband about matters of state. Melbourne had
urged her to 'tell him and show him everything connected with
public affairs', but this advice went unheeded. The Queen saw
her Ministers alone. Then the matter was solved simply by the
fact that the Queen became pregnant very shortly after her
marriage and found it necessary to run to the Prince for help
with her official work. The Prince was given his own key to the
government boxes after the birth of the Princess Royal in
November 1840. Greville noted the next year with the arrival
of the Prince of Wales:

I find . . . all the boxes and business are transmitted as usual to the
Palace, and the former opened and returned by the Prince . . . At first,
orders were given to the Foreign Office to send no more boxes . . . ; but
two days after, fresh orders were received to send the boxes as usual, and
to furnish the Prince with the necessary keys.[8]

Once established, the Prince's role as the Queen's secretary
grew year by year. His well-organized office, his genuine interest
in the classification of papers, his habit of making careful notes
on important interviews, and his practice of setting out his

39 The Prince Consort's Sitting Room at Windsor. From a photograph taken in 1860, and then hand-coloured. Some of the furniture came from Carlton House, and reflects the taste of the Prince formed by his father's collection of French furniture.

thoughts in extensive memoranda, make it easy for the later historian to follow his gradual assumption of this position. Fortunately the marriage was so successful that this was never resented by Queen Victoria, and indeed it is difficult to see how she could have carried out her duties with any other man as consort.

In a long and often quoted letter to the Duke of Wellington in 1850, he set out his understanding of his role – a most interesting and lucid 'job-description'. A queen regnant with a supportive spouse he suggests may even be in a stronger position than a king, but he goes on:

. . . this requires that the husband should entirely sink his *own individual* existence in that of his wife – that he should aim at no power by himself or for himself – should shun all contention – assume no separate responsibility before the public, but make his position entirely a part of hers – continually . . . watch every part of the public business, in order to be able to advise and assist her at any moment in any of the multifarious questions or duties brought before her, sometimes international,

sometimes political, or social or personal. As the natural head of her family, superintendent of her household, manager of her private affairs, sole *confidential* adviser in politics, only assistant in her communications with officers of Government, he is besides, the husband of the Queen, the tutor of the royal children, the private secretary of the sovereign, and her permanent minister.[9]

This lengthy description sets out the comprehensive and conscientious way in which he tackled his duties as the Queen's husband as he saw them. If we add to them his 'own' concerns, that is the philanthropic organizations and other projects, particularly South Kensington, it is not surprising that he died of overwork at 42. A sense of enormous strain comes through in his last years, in his reference to 'his treadmill' in a letter to Ernest, and to his 'true counterpart', the donkey in Carisbrooke Castle. 'He, too,' the Prince Consort wrote to his daughter Vicky in 1860, 'would rather munch thistles in the Castle Moat, than turn round the wheel . . . and small are the thanks he gets for his labour.'[10]

His habits of work were exemplary: his fondness for early rising meant that he got up at seven, winter or summer, often suffering from the chill of early-morning Windsor. At this hour he got through the government business, reading the papers, often drafting the Queen's reply or comments, in readiness for her approval. In addition, there were memoranda on all kinds of subjects, ranging from matters of state to the affairs of organizations in which he had a personal interest like the Horticultural Society or the 1851 Commission. The volume of paper was enormous — much of it drafted in his own hand. One historian has

PH—PPS THE FORTUNATE.
(As he Appeared when made a Knight of the Shower Bath.)

43 *PH PPS the Fortunate:* 'As he appeared when made Knight of the Shower Bath.' *Punch*, February 6, 1858.

Previous page, top
iii The town and the Coburg fortress from the Wustenmarner Hill, in 1820. Hand-coloured engraving by C. F. A. Richter, from the Kunstsammlungen Veste, Coburg.

Previous page, bottom
iv Detail from a view of the Veste Coburg from nearby the Bausenberg, 1837, with two young men, traditionally thought to be the Princes Ernest and Albert. Coloured lithograph by Friederich Rauser (1790–1856).

Opposite
v The Riesensaal in the Schloss Ehrenburg.

estimated that his memoranda on the Crimea alone ran to 50 volumes. In addition, he carried on a private correspondence with members of his large family. These were, of course, often of a political nature such as his correspondence with his younger cousin, Don Pedro of Portugal, to whom he wrote nearly every day. He concerned himself in the affairs of Coburg, partly because of Ernest's extravagance which led to continual calls on his time and money, but also because of his natural interest in his native Germany. After 1858, he wrote regularly to his daughter, Vicky, married to Fritz, the eldest son of the Prince Regent of Prussia.

Prince Albert valued this 'golden hour' with his papers before the Household was about. At breakfast he read the newspapers, marking them for the Queen's attention. He took his exercise in the form of an early walk with the Queen, or shooting or hunting, usually a brief excursion rather than the day's shooting more general amongst the English gentry. He was often attacked for his liking for shooting, but it was, in fact, a most necessary form of relaxation to a man who otherwise would have been overwhelmed even earlier by overwork and a broken constitution.[11]

Albert's greatest contribution to the history of England was indubitably the way in which he established the idea of a monarchy above party politics. This was a principle inculcated by Uncle Leopold early in life, and one to which Albert kept with enormous benefits to his wife and their descendants.

He was able to put his ideas into great practical effect when Melbourne's government fell in the summer of 1841, and Sir Robert Peel was called upon to form a Tory government. Peel was a man after the Prince's heart. Also reserved, upright, and somewhat stiff in his handling of people, he was the wealthy and enlightened son of a manufacturer from Staffordshire, a collector of pictures and a connoisseur. The Queen and the Prince visited Peel at Drayton Park on their 1843 tour, and Peel, like other ministers, stayed with the royal family in their different homes. He found Osborne House for them, and helped them in their efforts to improve Buckingham Palace. He supported projects like the 1851 Exhibition in which the Prince was keenly interested.

The Prince's support for Peel was demonstrated in the most obvious, indeed the only overt, partisan action he took in English domestic politics. He went down to the House of Commons to hear Peel speak on the Repeal of the Corn Laws, 'to mark the confidence of the Court'. This measure was of course, bitterly resented by the landed aristocracy to whom it appeared as an attack on agricultural prosperity. Lord George Bentinck, son of

44 *Grand entry of the Prince and Princess Frederick William of Prussia into Berlin* on February 8, 1858. The young couple were warmly welcomed in Berlin as they had been after their marriage in London. Their union fulfilled the Prince's lifelong dream of bringing England and Germany closer, but his hope of liberalizing Germany was defeated by the tragically short reign of his son-in-law.

the Duke of Portland, one of leaders of the Protectionist Tories, took the opportunity when replying to the debate to mount a virulent personal attack on the Prince, which prevented him ever attending the House of Commons again.

. . . I cannot but think that he listened to ill advice, when . . . *he allowed himself to be seduced by the first minister of the Crown* to come down to this house to usher in, to give *éclat*, and, as it were, by reflection from the Queen, to give the semblance of a personal sanction of her Majesty to a measure, which . . . a great majority of the landed aristocracy . . . imagine fraught with deep injury, if not ruin, to them . . .[12]

Albert's second great achievement was basically a service to the Crown — the establishment of the Household on a modern and efficient basis. This caused some complaints from disgruntled officers of state, who had lost their traditional perquisites. As Greville noted in 1848: 'The Q. and the Prince have taken to seize everything in the way of patronage they can lay their hands on. The Chamberlain formerly used to have it all, even to the appointment of domestic servants.'[13]

On the whole, domestic issues did not bring the court into conflict with the government. Despite the broadening of the franchise by the First Reform Bill of 1832, the governments of the next two decades were drawn largely from aristocratic circles. There was an occasional 'Israelitish philippic' from Disraeli, and, of course, both Peel and Gladstone came from solid mercantile backgrounds. Cobden and Bright brought a radical note into the Cabinet and the other bodies on which they served, but the Prime Ministers and the Foreign Secretaries of the period came from the greatest families in England, and were often related. These politicians might make common complaint about the interference of the Court, but there was rarely a real conflict of interest or attitude.

The only European conflict in which England was involved during Prince Albert's lifetime was the Crimean War, when England and France, traditionally enemies, found themselves allies defending Turkey against Russia. This led to a good deal of personal diplomacy: Napoleon III and his glamorous wife, Empress Eugenie, paid a state visit to England, and Queen Victoria and Prince Albert paid several visits to France, in 1855 and 1858. In September 1854, the Prince went by himself to France to visit the French army when on manoeuvres, an unusual expedition *en garcon* which the cartoonists picked up.

Outside the period of La Belle Alliance, relations with France were uneasy: in the 1840s the matter of the Spanish marriages had caused considerable friction. Relations with the more conservative governments of Europe – with Russia, Austria, Prussia and Saxony, with the Bourbon governments of Naples and Spain – caused some friction between the crown and the more liberal Foreign Ministers. The English public regarded such regimes as oppressive, and sympathy was on the whole on the side of their subjects particularly during and after the revolutions of 1848. Whatever the merits of the individual case, Queen Victoria was

45 Men of the Scots Fusilier Guards, wounded in the Crimea at Alma and Inkermann, March 1855. They were received at Buckingham Palace by the Queen and the Prince, who was a former Colonel of the Regiment.

always embarrassed by British insults to her fellow-sovereigns, or by hasty espousal by British ministers of revolutionary causes. Palmerston was a particular offender in the opinion of the royal couple, and there was continuing friction culminating in his resignation in 1851, for a premature congratulation to Louis Napoleon on his successful *coup d'etat*.

The 'Trent affair' at the end of the Prince's life indicates that his influence in foreign affairs was growing, and perhaps this is one of the unresolved questions about his early death — how much influence would he have brought to bear on foreign policy when he had become, in the words of Lytton Strachey, 'a man, grown grey in the service of the nation, virtuous, intelligent, and with the unexampled experience of a whole lifetime of government'.[14]

In no area of public life was Prince Albert's path potentially more thorny than in dealing with the army, but ironically it was an area in which his influence was very large.

During his lifetime in England the British army was in a state of eclipse: this has been described as a period of decline out of which it was only shaken by the successive traumatic shocks of the Crimean war and the Indian Mutiny. In fact, there seems to be a good deal of evidence that the thinking which ultimately led to the Cardwell reforms in the 1870s began in the 1840s with pressure for reform among officers with practical experience in the field. Civilian reformers were also interested but more generally in army reform as part of a wider sphere, such as administration and improvements in health and sanitation. In many of these movements, the Prince's influence can be seen, at first in a prominent manner which led to public comment. Later, he went about his work for the army in a more subtle way behind the scenes, an indication of his growing tactfulness. In addition, by the 1850s the English public was indulging in a pro-military phase and therefore appreciated his efforts.

Prince Albert enjoyed good relations with a number of senior officers, and with politicians concerned with army administration. The organization of the army at this period was archaic, with responsibility divided between at least two senior politicians: the Secretary for State for War and the Colonies was responsible for the size of the army, while the Secretary at War had responsibility for finances. Individual parts of the army came under the control of other departments: the Treasury managed the commissariat when the army went abroad; the Home Secretary was responsible for the Militia and Yeomanry and for the army in England. The Artillery and Engineers, and supplies for the army generally, arms, stores and barracks were administered by the Master General of the Ordinance; while promotion, discipline and training were a matter for the Commander-in-

Chief at the Horse Guards.

The resolution of these problems and the creation of a unified administration and command for the army was only achieved in the 1850s after the death of the Duke of Wellington. The Prince Consort's role in the reforms was small but important.[15] Both the Duke of Wellington and his successor Viscount Hardinge consulted him regularly about changes, and the Prince responded characteristically with a number of memoranda, many of which show an impressive grasp of the problems. He had a number of informal contacts with the army, one of them being through Colonel Charles Grey, a member of his Household from 1840, and his private secretary from 1849, whose brother, the third Earl Grey, was Secretary of State for War and the Colonies from 1846 to 1852. As in so many areas, the Prince seems to have been approached by enthusiastic reformers, and to have had the gift of espousing the right ideas and causes. He was concerned with the raising of a militia or volunteer reserve to supplement the regular army in the event of an invasion; with the movement to give line regiments territorial connections; with permanent depots in England, the provision of a permanent army headquarters and an adequate field day country at Aldershot; with military education in the shape of the Royal Military Academy at Sandhurst; with the founding of the Staff College; with the improvement of uniforms and equipment for both officers and men. He summoned Florence Nightingale to Balmoral to discuss army problems.

He was approached by the Duke of Wellington, in 1850, with the suggestion that he should be appointed Commander-in-Chief, a proposal which the Prince took seriously but wisely turned down in view of his existing heavy responsibilities as the Queen's private secretary.

Prince Albert's connection with the British army began in a most traditional fashion with his acceptance of the Colonelcy of one of the élite regiments of cavalry, the 11th Dragoon Guards, later the 11th Hussars. He took this seriously, drilling with this regiment and with others in both Hyde Park and Windsor Great Park, and learning the English words of command. Despite his lack of any formal military training, he seems to have enjoyed his contacts with the various regiments and with individual army officers.

Over the years he had added commands in other regiments, and he was of course painted in his various uniforms. Thus in 1842, he became Colonel of the Scots Fusilier Guards, as the Scots Guards were then called, and, in 1850, Colonel-in-Chief of the 60th, now the King's Royal Rifle Corps. In September 1852, on the death of the Duke of Wellington, he became Colonel of the Grenadier Guards, and Colonel-in-Chief of the Rifle Brigade. In 1843, he succeeded the Duke of Sussex as Colonel and Captain

THE "SATISFACTION" OF A "GENTLEMAN."

General of the Honorable Artillery Company, effectively the City of London volunteers. He kept these last three appointments till death; and, as usual, he played more than the passive role of a titular chief.

In 1843 the tragic case of Colonel Fawcett, who was called out and killed by his brother-in-law Lieutenant Munro, concentrated public attention on the practice of duelling among officers in the British army. The Prince took the matter up with the Duke of Wellington, and suggested that Courts of Honour should be established on the pattern which had proved effective in the Bavarian army. The dilemma was considerable as the Prince observed in a letter to Wellington. Since 'this unchristian and barbarous custom had been generally condemned, forbidden by law and severely punished; but no substitute has been granted', the officer was left with the alternative of breaking the law or 'of losing caste in the estimate of his profession'.

In due course, the Prince's persistence had its way: the matter was discussed by the Cabinet, and Amended Articles of War were published. These proclaimed that it was: 'suitable to the character of honourable men to apologise and offer redress for wrong or insult committed', and this virtually ended duelling in the army. There were occasional instances of 'affairs of honour' over the next decade but these were, as it were, optional: there was no further obligation on an officer to call out an opponent.[16]

The Prince's next venture into military affairs had a less flattering outcome. The British army had been using a broad-topped shako on the continental pattern since Waterloo, but by 1840 a

48 *Prince Albert's Studio: Punch* found the Prince's preoccupation with uniform irresistible. This is a sketch for the *Punch* cartoon. A prototype of the hat designed by the Prince was made, and happily has survived.

general desire for a headdress somewhat lighter and less cumbersome combined with the government's perennial desire for economy to institute changes in both uniform and headgear. The changes in uniform had to wait for 1853, when the clothing system of the army was reformed, and colonels were no longer responsible for providing uniforms for the men under their command. The headdress however, was the subject of discussions between the Prince and the Duke of Wellington in August 1843. The following month a circular memorandum from the Horse Guards announced that Her Majesty had been pleased to approve: 'a hat of a new form for infantry . . . which is considered more adapted to [their] convenience and comfort than the chaco hithertoo in use.'

This hat was conical with a brim, and its appearance provoked: 'a violent attack upon the Prince in the newspapers etc. respecting the new military head dress' apparently leading him to conclude that: 'there are many ill-disposed people'.

The *Illustrated London News* published a drawing of it and pronounced it: 'neither soldierlike nor appropriate'. In December the same journal announced that the new cap had been so disapproved that a new one was to be substituted. Although this was: 'more soldierlike than its predecessor, it is we think still of somewhat tasteless design'. However it was duly adopted, and the 'Albert Shako' was in use up till the Crimean War.[17]

The new helmet for the Household Cavalry chosen in 1843 and based on the Prussian cavalry helmet, 'handsome, light, and convenient', according to one observer, was also called after the Prince, and as the 'Albert Helmet', survived until the changes of 1855.

The original hat might have been rejected by the Horse Guards, but it was enthusiastically adopted by *Punch* which used it frequently to lampoon the Prince throughout the next ten years.

The Prince was also concerned some ten years later when the uniforms of the army were finally changed in response to a mounting dissatisfaction with the soldiers' dress, particularly with the short coatee, which gave little protection against the weather, and the stiff leather stocks and other inconvenient and archaic items of clothing. In April 1853 the army clothing contractors, Messrs. Isaac Campbell and Co. of St. James's Street, called to submit the patterns of uniforms, accoutrements etc., as approved by the Commander-in-Chief. Research was done at many levels into both foreign uniforms and foreign equipment. Prince Albert asked his brother Duke Ernest to provide a: 'Prussian needle gun from Erfurt', and it was on his advice that the British ambassador in Vienna was asked to provide a complete set of Austrian equipment.

49 The Military Review – The Camp at Chobham. The troops returning to their encampment after a Field Day, 1853. Lithograph by Edmund Walker after Louis Haghe.

A number of different patterns of uniform were taken to the Chobham camp, and 'modelled' by officers and men of the different regiments, and the wearers asked for their reactions. Prolonged discussion followed. The correspondence between Windsor and the Horse Guards reveals the interest taken by the Prince, both in the details of the uniform, its practicality and convenience, and also in the cost and the quality of the different cloths suggested. It was not till the autumn of 1854 that the different pattern uniforms were 'approved and sealed'. The changes were embodied in the 1855 Dress Regulations issued in April 1855. The Prince was painted in the new uniform that year.

The interest in weapons continued; in 1861 the Prince was in correspondence with Palmerston, urging the advantages of a breechloading rifle, and discussing the problems of replacing the 400,000 muskets then in use throughout the armed forces.

For the cavalry, a helmet was intended to replace the shako, but the Horse Guards found this a difficult problem: 'ingenuity has been taxed', they admitted. A new pattern of helmet was designed, and an officer dispatched to the Crimea to test reaction. He called on Lord Raglan, wearing it, and was immediately challenged by a sentry who thought he was a Russian officer because of the resemblance to the enemy's headgear! This so alarmed both the army and the Queen and the Prince that, when the headdress came to them for final approval, the helmet was rejected in favour of a new light shako.[18]

One of the problems that faced British commanders was that there was little opportunity to gain experience in commanding troops in the field.

In 1847, provoked by an invasion scare, the Prince wrote to Wellington suggesting 'a concentration of a part of our land forces in England for a short time'. He also pointed out that any such concentration would be dependent on the railway, '. . . an

operation which is comparatively new and will want some practice and experience before it can be satisfactorily performed'.[19]

He proposed a camp in the south of England, either on
Salisbury Plain or at Winchester or at Bagshot. The idea was
turned down by Wellington on the grounds of cost, but taken up
by Hardinge on his appointment in 1852. The result was the
'camp of exercise' held at Chobham from June to August 1853.
The Prince and Hardinge corresponded over many of the details,
and appear to have chosen the commander Lord Seaton in consultation.

The main object was, in Hardinge's words: 'to accustom the
Officers, and Troops to move over rough and undulating ground
. . . take up ground in reference to its shape for defensive purposes
or to attack a position by such combination of three arms . . .'
However, he also saw it as an opportunity to test out new equipment from carts for the commissariat to knapsacks, muskets and
uniform.

Popular prints of the period underline the public relations
value of this exercise. Hardinge instructed that the public should
be allowed 'the most liberal freedom of the Camp, to make it as
popular as the Exhibition'. The Queen accompanied by the
Prince and the Duke and Duchess of Coburg, inspected the camp
on June 21 after the troops had had a week to settle in; the
Prince returned to exercise with 'his brigade (Guards)', but went
down with measles a week later, caught from his children. The
entire royal family was prostrate and the Queen and the Prince
could only return briefly at the end to spend two days with the
second draft of troops. Nonetheless, the Queen wrote proudly to
Uncle Leopold of:

our dear camp . . . When I think that this camp, and all our large fleet,
are without doubt the result of Albert's assiduous and unceasing representations to the late and present Government, . . . one may be proud
and thankful, but as usual, he is so modest that he allows no praise . . .[20]

The camp exposed a number of deficiencies in training and
equipment, but was such a successful innovation that, by August,
plans were being laid by Hardinge and Prince Albert for the purchase of a permanent area for a regular camp of exercise. Land
at Aldershot was chosen because of its excellent strategic position
as a railway centre and, spurred on by the threat of enclosure,
Prince Albert persuaded Gladstone to provide funds for the purchase of an initial 3,000 acres.

This was supplemented by further purchases until 1861, but
the land was used not so much for a 'camp of exercise' as for
permanent army quarters. This was partly due to the need for
better facilities but the initiative may have come from the Prince
who suggested to Hardinge that one way to ensure the retention

50 *Mr Punch receiving the Victoria Cross.*
The Victoria Cross was instituted as an
award for bravery in the British Army in
1857, partly to meet the need for individual
acts of bravery where there was no suitable
campaign medal. The Prince was personally
concerned with the design.

of the land was to put buildings on it.[21]

One of the buildings was the Royal Pavilion, a fairly capacious
'hut' provided for the accommodation of the Queen and members
of the royal family when attending field days and reviews.
Initially rooms were provided for the royal children to accompany their parents. The pavilion remained in royal occupation
until the second World War. It was only demolished in the
1960s.

The British army suffered throughout the period from inadequate
financing. This was due to the traditional parsimony of the
Treasury, which kept defence-spending pared back, and also to
the English mistrust of a 'standing army', a fear which dated
back to the days of the Stuarts. Except in moments of invasion-
scare, a low army budget was one way to keep public spending
down.

There was an arrogant assumption that, since the British army
had emerged triumphant from Waterloo, there was little need to
fear for the defence of England. National defence was seen pri-
marily as a matter for the navy, about which the English have
always felt more warmly. Continental standing armies, raised on
a regular conscription basis, led by better educated officers who
obtained their commissions by examination rather than by purchase, better equipped and better trained, were seen as no threat
to liberal Englishmen.

This complacency was first shaken by belligerent gestures on
the part of Louis Philippe in 1847, and Louis Napoleon's coup
d'état in 1851 finally aroused the British government to action.
Lord John Russell laid a Militia Bill before parliament, provoking

51 Launch of the *Royal Albert* by the
Queen, May 13, 1854. From a watercolour
by J. W. Carmichael in the Royal Collection.
The Queen was much moved by the ship
'bearing my beloved Lord and Master's
name and his portrait'. This was an
up-to-date screw steamer, sister ship to the
Duke of Wellington, 120 guns and 272 feet
in length. The concern about national
defence in the 1850s led to naval
rearmament.

the comment from Prince Albert that this was the third time in
the Queen's reign that such a crisis had arisen, and asking in the
Queen's name for further details of military and naval strength
and the proposed increases. When, nine months later, the Duke
of Wellington died, leaving the post of Commander-in-Chief
vacant, the opportunity for reform in the army was presented to
an administration already concerned about invasion. The traditional English superiority at sea was being effectively ended by
the use of steamships. No longer would an invading force have
to wait for a fair wind; the whole south coast now lay open to an
enemy with a larger army. The British army averaged about
100,000, compared with a French army of 400,000, an Austrian army of over 600,000 and a Prussian army of 325,000.[20]
Excluding India, the British force had to garrison and protect
British territories from Hong-Kong to the Caribbean, including
the Cape (South Africa), Ceylon, Western Australia, Malta and
the Ionian Islands, and Trinidad and St. Helena.

The government was concerned to make the army more effec-
tive for home defence and also to provide some form of 'Home
Guard' which would be an improvement on the traditional
Militia and Volunteers raised in the Napoleonic period. This new

force achieved considerable public support by 1860 with the Volunteer movement, in which the Prince took a great personal interest.

Both the Volunteers and the related Rifle Corps received considerable impetus from the knowledge that France was increasing her armed forces, brought vividly home to the Queen and the Prince on their visit to Cherbourg in 1858, and by the invasion scare of 1859. Public reaction was swift; the Prince wrote to Stockmar:

... people think of nothing else but measures of protection against an Ally; Volunteer Corps are being formed in all the towns. The lawyers of the Temple go through regular drill. Lords Spencer, Abercorn, Elcho, etc., are put through their pacings in Westminster Hall by gaslight in the same rank and file with shopkeepers. Close on 50,000 are already under arms.[22]

Though the crisis passed, public interest continued. Large reviews of Volunteers were held in both London and Edinburgh in the summer of 1860. In July 1860, the National Rifle Association held its first meeting at Wimbledon, when the Queen fired the first symbolic shot, loyally stage-managed to ensure a bull's eye.

The original instructions to Lords Lieutenant, sent out by the government in May 1859, had been based on a comprehensive

52 *The First Shot at Wimbledon*. The Queen opening the first meeting of the Volunteer Rifle Corps at Wimbledon, July 2, 1860. From a lithograph by A. Maclure.

memorandum by the Prince and submitted to the Cabinet two days before. This had emphasized the role of Volunteers in carrying out defensive operations, for which guerilla activity and skill in marksmanship were important.

The movement had its critics in England and abroad. The *New York Herald* reported Cobden's remark to an American in Paris: 'as for Prince Albert's Rifle mania, that is mere Germanism, in the disguise of British patriotism'.[23] However, it is important to emphasize that the Prince in all his comments on the movement stresses its *voluntary* nature, an element which was markedly absent in Prussian and other continental armies. In an enthusiastic letter to his brother, from Aldershot in May 1860, he lists the numbers enlisted as volunteers, some 124,000 to be increased by a naval and coastguard reserve and by yeomanry:

... they show the greatest enthusiasm for their work, as the English generally do, when they undertake something. They also look very well, just like gentlemen soldiers. From a military point of view, they are rather awkward, but differ from the peasant recruit or the militia man who comes from the working class ... The remarkable thing is that in the army, navy, militia, reserve they are all volunteers ... .[24]

The subordination of the military to the civil power was again emphasized by the Prince in his address to the Grenadier Guards on the occasion of their 200th anniversary. Having reminded them of the regiment's battle honours, its loyalty to the sovereign even in periods of national division, and of their volunteer status, he congratulated the regiment on its record of living: '... in the midst of all the temptations of a luxurious metropolis without loss in vigour and energy — ... in harmony and good fellowship with its brother citizens ... .'[25]

Military education at all levels concerned a number of reformers throughout the 1840s. Sidney Herbert, Secretary at War, in 1844–1846, and later known as Florence Nightingale's ally in the post-Crimean reforms, had concerned himself with army schools and with the screening of candidates for officers' commissions. Entry to the army at this period was either by purchase of a commission, or through the Royal Military Academy Sandhurst which was the subject of an unfavourable report in 1855. Education for senior officers intended for positions on the staff was even more lamentable. Again comparison with continental countries showed that England lagged in military education as in technical and industrial. Thus while the English spent £1,300 annually, Prussia spent £26,000, France £48,000 and Austria over £100,000.

The Prince's role was discreet but significant, as a modern historian of the army has described. 'Keenly interested in the practicalities of staff work, he worked behind the scenes, pressing the case for a staff corps to train subordinate officers and for a staff of competent generals and officers.'[26] It is a tragic irony that his last public engagement was a visit to inspect the new buildings at Sandhurst for the new Staff College and the Royal Military Academy, on November 22, 1861.

A more publicized and individual effort for Army Education was the building and endowment of the Prince Consort's Library at Aldershot. Designed by Francis Fowke, the Engineer Officer, responsible for so much in South Kensington, it was constructed at the Prince's expense, and opened in September 1860. The Library itself, which included both historic works on strategy and tactics, as well as modern military manuals, biographies and more general histories, maps, and works on uniforms, drill and weapons, was collected and purchased by the Prince. Until his death the Library and a librarian were maintained at his expense. The regulations for the use and running of the Library make it clear how personal an interest the Prince took in even minor details. The building itself survives with part of its collection, amid the redeveloped cantonments of Aldershot town.

53 Oil sketch for a portrait of the Queen, by Sir Francis Grant.

CHAPTER FOUR

Albert the Good

Prince Albert came to England at the beginning of a period of great intellectual ferment paralleled in more practical fields by an interest in administrative and social reform. The 1840s and 1850s saw the setting up of a number of influential pressure groups which brought about much needed changes in many areas of national life.

In education these years saw the reform of the ancient universities of Oxford and Cambridge: the modernization of the curriculum, the admission of non-Anglicans, the breaking down of the ancient practices and customs which kept them the province of elderly and often idle professors. A new Irish university was founded, on non-sectarian lines to compete with the exclusively Anglican Trinity College, Dublin, while the whole South Kensington project was to contribute to the teaching of both science and art. The older public schools were reformed, and were supplemented by others like Wellington College, founded in memory of the Great Duke. Primary education did not become compulsory in England until the 1870s but the increased interest in voluntary schools, such as the National Schools, foreshadowed the moment when the government would have to take responsibility for the education of the nation.

Housing reform, like education, was still seen as a matter for voluntary effort. A number of societies made themselves responsible for building experimental blocks of dwellings for the respectable poor; concerned themselves with pensions for domestic servants; interested themselves in temperance movements, in improved methods of sewage disposal, in public health generally. The Prince was President of a number of these bodies, and in many of them he played a most active role. In addition, at Osborne and Balmoral, and as Ranger of Windsor Great Park, he showed himself to be a dedicated and benevolent landlord, taking thought intelligently for the quality of life of those working for him.

Enthusiasts for reform turned to him not only for his patronage and the prestige of the royal name, but also for practical advice. An early advocate of the Temperance Coffee house, John Clabon, has left an account of one such visit. He had written a pamphlet on *Leisure-houses for the Poor* dealing with the problem of providing an economic and attractive alternative to the public-house, and called on the Prince at Windsor to discuss it. He saw the Prince in his secretary's room, 'a little room, businesslike, with a large office table and directories, and so on — everything very comfortable and handsome . . . Presently the Prince was announced. I was introduced; he shook hands with Lord Torrington, and established himself with his back to the fire and hands behind him in true English fashion, we three standing before him . . .' The Prince's advice was brisk and positive: he

55 *Prince Albert 'at Home':* 'When He will sustain (no end of) different characters.' *Punch* published this view of the polymath Prince in March 1847. It includes him as sportsman, designer, soldier and Chancellor of Cambridge University.

PRINCE ALBERT "AT HOME."
WHEN HE WILL SUSTAIN (NO END OF) DIFFERENT CHARACTERS.

suggested that the coffee houses must be economic and run by people of good character to whom the magistrates would grant licences, he advocated that they should be welcoming to women and children, and even that smoking should not be restricted to smoking rooms, but allowed throughout. Mr. Clabon proposed to introduce an occasional dance, strictly temperance in character, the Prince 'doubted whether they would enjoy it or enter upon it with spirit, unless they had something to drink', observing that at Balmoral the staff expected whisky, and even at Osborne strong beer was required for a good party.[1]

He was not a mere figurehead. Thus he refused initially to become a Freeman of two of the Great City Companies, the Fishmongers and the Goldsmiths, because they were traditionally connected with political parties.[2] When he and the Queen went to Ireland on their visit in 1849, they deliberately omitted the Deaf and Dumb Institution in Belfast, an overtly sectarian organization, and the royal bounty given on that occasion was very carefully distributed to the least divisive bodies.[3]

The Prince's first address was to the Society for the Abolition of Slavery, on June 1, 1840, and on this occasion he wrote his speech in German, translated it and learnt it off by heart. Subsequent speeches came more easily but, though delivery was more fluent, he still worried both about the content and about actually making the speech in public. The Queen complained that their visit to Cherbourg in 1858 was overshadowed by the Prince's attacks of nerves over his speech.

The philanthropic society for which he did most in a practical way was the Society for Improving the Condition of the Labour-

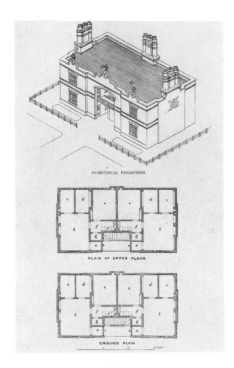

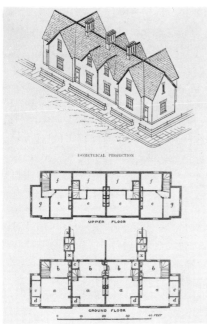

56 *Top:* Model cottages, designed for the poor and erected in Hyde Park in 1851 during the Great Exhibition. They were dismantled and re-erected in Kennington Park. *Bottom:* Model cottages erected by the Royal Windsor Society.

ing Classes, of which he became President in 1844. This Society, recognizing the lack of decent housing for the working classes in London and other large towns, set themselves to commission designs for sanitary modern buildings which could be erected cheaply. Their architect was Henry Roberts, a man who specialized in this field, and produced some very interesting plans, remarkable not only for their cheapness, but also for radical planning based on research into the needs of families, and the most up-to-date thinking on hygiene and health. The Society put up some lodging houses for single men, always a problem with London's large immigrant population, and then turned to the more difficult problem of providing housing fit for families. The Prince used his position as President of the Commissioners for the Exhibition of 1851 to persuade the Duke of Wellington to make available vacant ground near the Hyde Park Barracks for the erection of a pair of cottages to Roberts's design. These provided accommodation for two families, very adequately by contemporary standards, and were seen by thousands during the Exhibition, including builders, developers, landowners and responsible employers in industrial towns. A number of houses exactly to the design were built, but many more must have been influenced by it – the hollow bricks for improved insulation and damp-proofing, the hard-wearing hygienic finishes, the provision of water and internal sanitation, the allocation of separate bedrooms for children of different sexes, the emphasis on fresh air for good health. After the Exhibition the cottages were dismantled and re-erected in Kennington, on Duchy of Cornwall land, where they can be seen today at the entrance to Kennington Park.[4]

Another pair still stands in Windsor, where they were erected by the Royal Windsor Improvement Society, another organization in which the Prince took an interest. This gave prizes to the houseproud, which were distributed at the annual fair. This Association continued under the patronage of the royal family long after the Prince's death.[5]

The Prince's burden of public engagements was heavy, since he was involved both as deputy for the Queen and increasingly in his own right. He was present at many of the most memorable events of the period, at occasions which marked scientific and engineering advances, improvements in hygiene and medicine and in care for the sick. He took an interest in scientific matters over and above the call of official duty. He was present at the launching of the *Great Britain*; he opened the Royal Albert Bridge at Saltash, the last work of the dying Brunel; he spoke at the opening of the New City Cattle Market in Islington; he laid innumerable first stones, and declared untold institutions open, including the Albert Dock in Liverpool, and the Royal Exchange

57 The opening of the Coal Exchange, City of London, October 30, 1849. From the Stationer's *Almanack*. The Queen was intended to perform the ceremony but in fact the Prince did it on her behalf, supported by his two eldest children.

and the Coal Exchange in the City of London. Among the foundation stones which he laid were those of the Chest Hospital, Brompton (1844); St. Mary's, Paddington (1845); Portsmouth, Gosport and Southsea Hospital (1847); City of London Chest Hospital (1851); Reigate Asylum (1853); Seamen's Hospital, Dock Street, London (1846); Chapel of Ease, Eton (1852); St. Thomas's Church, Newport, Isle of Wight (1854), with full masonic honours. He also laid the first stones for Homes for Seamen in London and Liverpool (1846) and for a Home for Strangers, in this case 'oriental strangers who visit this country', who would be offered 'a comfortable and respectable lodging, with wholesome food, at a cost which it is presumed that they can afford . . .' (June 1856). He opened the Royal Medical Benevolent College for 'decayed medical men and their widows', the Home for Soldiers' Daughters in Hampstead (1858), a by-product of the Crimean War; and did not disdain to have the Albert Wing of the Licensed Victuallers' Asylum called after him.

A fairly full picture is given by the pages of the *Illustrated London News*; it leaves to the imagination the full burden of his public work, the constant exposure to public pressure, the lobbying of local worthies, the sheer weight of engagements, the travelling by coach and train often to return the same day since the Queen did not like him to stay away. Very occasionally he complained: 'I am still worse off,' he wrote to Ernest in 1855. 'In the morning I have to be present at the inauguration of a hospital, and in the evening I have to preside at a dinner in Trinity House,

which will last five hours and where I have to hear six addresses.'[6]

But it was not all public addresses. It was the ballast-heavers of Trinity House who benefited from his intervention over the previous 'truck system' by which work was allocated through the public-houses, necessitating the men spending time and money in pubs to get work. As they themselves recalled:

We appealed to men of all classes, and opened an office ourselves; but we got no real help till we sent an appeal [to the Prince as new Master of Trinity House]. He at once listened to us. He could put himself down from the throne he shared to the wretched home of us poor men, and could feel what we and our wives and children were suffering from the terrible truck-driving system . . .

The relief was immediate: the Prince saw the President of the Board of Trade and arranged for an additional clause in a Merchant Shipping Act then going through Parliament which gave Trinity House the control of the ballast-heavers in the Port of London.[7]

This incident was typical of many where his position enabled him to intervene to end some abuse or to bring about some much-needed reform. As Cecil Woodham-Smith has pointed out, the Queen was not greatly 'concerned with improvement of the conditions in which a great mass of her subjects passed their lives. She lived through an age of profound social change but neither public health, nor housing, nor the education of her people, nor their representation, engaged much of her time'.[8] The Prince was, therefore, a particularly valuable partner to the Queen, in the way in which he demonstrated the royal couple's interest in philanthropic matters, as well as in the help he gave in shouldering the sheer weight of public engagements.

Towards the end of his life he found himself chairing a number of gatherings of eminent scientific and academic figures who had come to recognize him as the supporter of scientific advance. This recognition gave him great pleasure, though he found the strain of addressing such gatherings considerable.

Thus he was President of the British Association at their meeting in Aberdeen in 1859. In his address he took the opportunity of reminding the 'travelling philosophers' and others of what the highlands had to offer, of wild plants and animals being gradually driven out of other parts of the country, of the advances in modern technology like the telescope and modern rifles which aided the sportsman, of the sturdy natives of Aberdeen, 'presenting a happy mixture of the Celt, Goth, Saxon and Dane'. In a long speech he praised the Association which provided in England the one umbrella-organization for scientific studies, something, he pointed out, which was done overseas by a government-backed academy or university. He also expressed

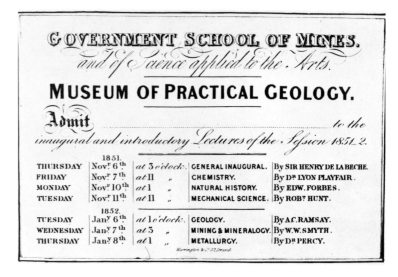

60 Invitation to the opening series of lectures of the Museum of Practical Geology, 1851. This museum was founded by Sir Henry de la Beche, on very utilitarian principles. Prince Albert became patron and, in due course, it amalgamated with the College of Science, providing accommodation for evening lectures often attended by the Prince. Eventually, the scientific side of the institution moved to South Kensington, to become the forerunner of Imperial College.

61 *The Prince Consort delivering the inaugural address to the British Association* in Aberdeen, in September 1859. He had accepted the office of President as 'a representative of that large public, which profits by and admires your exertions . . .' and a means of the Queen's testifying to you, 'through . . . her husband, that your labours are not unappreciated by your Sovereign'.

his own 'satisfaction that there should exist bodies of men who will bring the . . . wants of science before the public and the Government, who will even hand round the begging box and expose themselves . . . to rebuffs . . . with the certainty besides, of being considered great bores.'

The scientists were asked to Balmoral at the end of the meeting, being entertained with pipe music and 'athletic games, in which,' the Prince told his brother, 'they are not expected to take an active part.'

He found even more satisfaction in the chairing of an international conference on statistics in 1860, in which his old tutor and life-long correspondent, M. Quetelet, took part. The Statistical Congress of All Nations was founded after the Great Exhibition and, as the Prince reminded his audience, the study of statistics was the foundation of modern progress, since without accurate

Right

62 The Prince was enthusiastic about the new science of statistics. This contemporary card shows him as the centre of the British Empire.

knowledge, advances in health, scientific knowledge and government administration were impossible.

Often he took the opportunity given by a public appearance to put forward some idea or project about which he felt deeply. One such occasion was the National Education Conference of 1857, where he addressed the delegates in a very outspoken manner. He reminded them of the problem that half the children in the country went untutored despite the increase in educational facilities since the beginning of the century, that the problem was clear but

the common object has been contemplated from the most different points of view and pursued often upon antagonistic principles. Some have sought the aid of Government, others that of the Church to which they belong; some have declared it to be the duty of the State to provide elementary instruction for the people at large, others have seen in the State interference a check to the spontaneous extertions of the people themselves; some, again, have advocated a plan of compulsory education based upon local self-government, others the voluntary system . . . [differences] in the religious field have not been less marked and potent.

He would not have been present, he told the delegates bluntly,

63

if they had not agreed to leave their differences behind and meet on neutral ground.[9]

This conference dealt with the problems of primary education, but he was more concerned with higher education, from the provision of what we would today call polytechnic education at South Kensington, through the problems of university curriculi both at Cambridge and in Ireland, to the equally pressing problem of 'on the job' training for officers and diplomats. Neither of these careers was recruited by examination, the army being by purchase, the diplomatic by patronage. The Prince suggested in 1855 that entry to the diplomatic should be by competitive examination, followed by a later exam to assess the recruit's progress: 'This principle has the great advantage of keeping a young man at work (and at a *mental* not mere clerk's work) at a time of life when his habits for the future are being formed, and this also will keep him out of many a scrape.' He found it necessary to emphasize the need of good languages, not only German, French and Latin 'being the 3 roots of the English language . . . in my opinion indispensable for a thorough understanding of it, particularly as it possesses no definite grammar of its own'. Latin would help with the acquisition of Italian, Portuguese and Spanish. Also necessary, he maintained, were Russian and Turkish, to impress on the young man 'that it is his first duty to become acquainted with the country to which he is sent, which however is absolutely impossible if he does not understand the language.'[10] Entrance exams to both the army and the diplomatic service had to wait till many years after his death, largely because of the distrust felt by the aristocratic English establishment of men recruited by such methods.

He found the universities of Oxford and Cambridge unsatisfactory in their methods of government and in the range of subjects they offered. Even after the reforms of the 1850s he could observe to the loyal citizens of Birmingham, when he laid the foundation stone of the Midland Institute:

No human pursuits make any material progress until science is brought to bear upon them . . . The study of the laws by which the Almighty governs the Universe is therefore our bounden duty. Of these laws our great academies and seats of education have, rather arbitrarily, selected only two spheres or groups . . . as essential parts of our national education; the laws which regulate quantities and proportions, which form the subject of mathematics, and the laws regulating the expression of our thoughts, that is to say, grammar . . . These laws are most important branches of knowledge, their study trains and elevates the mind, but they are not the only ones . . .

There were also he pointed out logic and metaphysics, physiology and psychology, which governed human beings, both body and soul, and 'those which govern human society, and the

63 Prince Albert was inaugurated as Chancellor of Cambridge University on March 25, 1847, by a deputation of the Vice-Chancellor and other leading figures who waited on him in London.

relations between man and man (the subjects of politics, jurisprudence, and politic economy)'. He advised Birmingham to specialize in 'the laws regulating matter and form . . . and to follow with undivided attention chiefly the sciences of mechanics, physics and chemistry, and the fine arts in painting, sculpture, and architecture.'[11]

The university with which he was most closely associated was Cambridge, to which he was recruited by Whewell, Master of Trinity, and others, chiefly for the mistaken notion that the Queen's husband would protect the university from the hostile winds of change which were beginning to blow. The Chancellor of Cambridge, the Duke of Northumberland, died in February 1847, and Prince Albert was approached to become the next Chancellor. Despite the challenge presented by Lord Powys, a backwoods peer, the Prince stood against him, won by a narrow margin, and was duly installed, the university authorities calling on him at Buckingham Palace. The contest delighted *Punch*, which promptly suggested that the Prince would now stand for election as Lord Mayor.[12]

The Prince pressed ahead with a discreet programme of reform. First, he obtained a 'comprehensive table, showing the scheme of tuition separately and in the University . . . I mean the subjects to be taught in the different colleges, the authors to be read there, the subjects for examination, those selected for competition and prizes, and the lectures to be given by the different professors in their different branches . . .'[13] Then, armed with suggestions from Whewell, he consulted Peel and others on desirable reforms. Acting in conjunction with two successive Vice-Chancellors, he finally achieved substantial changes in the curriculum, passed by the Senate on October 31, 1848. Even *Punch* applauded. These, first, made it incumbent on those pursuing the existing Tripos of classics and mathematics to attend at least one term of lectures in one of 14 subjects new to Cambridge examinees, including modern history, law, philosophy, and a large number of scientific subjects. Two new Triposes were established, one in the moral sciences, that is in philosophy, modern history, law and jurisprudence, and one in the natural sciences, anatomy, physiology, chemistry, botany and geology.

By these reforms, Cambridge had hoped to avoid the establishment of a Royal Commission, but the changes were nothing like enough to satisfy the real radicals. The Royal Commission was established and again the Prince's influence was used in the cause of reform to persuade the Cambridge authorities to co-operate.

In due course the Royal Commission finished its work, giving a much needed modern constitution to the two older universities, establishing new Schools of study, giving the university more

H.R.H. FIELD-MARSHAL CHANCELLOR PRINCE ALBERT TAKING THE PONS ASINORUM.

64 *H.R.H. Field-Marshal Chancellor Prince Albert taking the Pons Asinorum.* The scheme of reform endorsed by the Prince was passed by the Senate of Cambridge University on October 31.

authority over the colleges, and endowing new professorships to encourage wider studies among the undergraduates. Through a series of correspondents, first Dr. Philpott, then Dr. Lightfoot, and through the Professor of Geology, Adam Sedgwick, the Prince kept in touch with university thought and gossip. In his characteristic way, first he learnt from his informants, then he gradually made his own suggestions. The men who had resented 'the student of Saxe-Gotha'[14] gradually recognized the worth of their Chancellor. In the words of Professor Chadwick, Cambridge 'came to admire the steady and prudent benevolence of the man; never sentimental, never up in the clouds, always practical in his quest for the better, and, despite the reserve and the dignity, content to do good by stealth and without desire to take public credit for what he achieved.'[15]

An even thornier subject was the setting up of a new Irish university to supplement the Ascendancy-based Trinity College, Dublin, open only to members of the Episcopalian established Church of Ireland, excluding both the nonconformist North, and the Roman Catholic majority in the rest of the country. The proposal was for a single university with three constituent colleges, in Cork, Galway and Belfast; this arrangement raised a number of issues including the balance between university and college ability to control the entry of students, the granting of degrees, and the control of standards. There was a desire to avoid provincial and religious prejudice as far as possible in such a deeply divided country, and to raise the standing of the colleges in their own neighbourhoods without depriving the university of national character and influence.

The matter was under discussion in 1849, the year of a successful but all too rare royal visit to Ireland. It was referred to Prince Albert for his advice, Shaw Lefevre observing to Lord Clarendon, Lord Lieutenant of Ireland, 'Our Cambridge Chancellor Prince Albert will give as sound an opinion on the question as can be desired.'[16]

The Prince's suggestions were practical and modern: that to the curriculum, already wider than those of other universities in the British Isles at that time, should be added civil engineering and agriculture, both important for their contribution to the Irish economy. This was a matter in which he had already shown interest, having given his patronage to an Irish agricultural College.

He also suggested that scholarships should be given in the 'Irish language', a subject he suggested would be more happily called the 'Celtic Language', in view of its links with other tongues such as Cornish and Breton. The reaction to this was interesting since the Board thought that the teaching of Celtic, 'now limited to the mere peasantry on one hand and the Antiquaries', would encourage its revival as a living language and might prove divisive and a discouragement to the learning of modern languages. But the Prince also suggested that scholarships should be given to encourage students in the schools of modern languages, geography and modern history. Lord Clarendon revealed with some embarrassment that there was so little common ground on modern history that a common textbook would be difficult to find. He added that a Chair of History had only recently been established and then only 'to the regret of Dr. Murray and the Roman Catholic Bishops'. It was perhaps optimistic or naïve of the Prince to put forward his rational modern suggestions in a situation so deeply torn by sectarian divisions, but they show his usual practical good sense.

As usual he took advice, both from Peel and from Lord Clarendon, the man on the spot; he also looked carefully into the matter, taking the opportunity of his visit to Belfast to discuss both the choice of professors and the 'plan of studies'. His experiences at Cambridge had already made him wary of ceding too much power from the university, the centralizing, degree-giving body which would set the standards for the component parts, for the colleges. In this case the danger was not the traditional lethargic independence of the Cambridge combination room but a more profound division: '. . . if left to themselves the Colleges would degenerate in the South into Roman Catholic seminaries and in the North into a Presbyterian school.'[17]

The problems of the Queen's University were those of Ireland itself: though the Prince's suggestions pointed up these problems, they were beyond his wit to solve.

He showed a very considerable interest in Ireland, both in the encouragement of agricultural research and then in his patronage of the Dublin Exhibition of 1853. He saw the need for prosperity, for the encouragement of both agriculture and industry in the island. Whether, had he lived, the Queen would have established yet another royal home in Ireland, as was advocated, it is difficult to say. Had there been an Irish home as well as one in the Highlands, perhaps the problems of Ireland would have received more attention and even a degree of solution.

65 *The Hero of a Hundred Portraits*. A view of the young prince by Phiz. (Hablot Knight Browne, 1815–82.)

CHAPTER FIVE

The Prince
as Patron of the Arts

When parliament cut back the Prince's annual grant from £50,000 to £30,000 he wrote to Stockmar that his only regret was that he would be prevented from giving as much help as he would like to artists and men of learning and science.[1] This was not a vapid or presumptuous remark from the 20-year-old Prince; he was, in fact, through example and official encouragement as much as through immediate patronage and purchase, to become a most important figure in the collecting world of the 1840s and 1850s.

He was a frequent visitor to artist's studios, interesting himself in their work as well as purchasing a number of works by living artists. T. S. Cooper, writing some 25 years after the Prince's death remembered the time when 'the Prince Consort came forward as a patron, and did everything in his power for the furtherance and advancement of art generally, as well as of all other branches of science and learning. Truly he was a good and great man, and his influence was felt in England for many years after he was taken from us.'[2]

Of course, as the husband of the sovereign, he was in a position where artistic patronage was expected of him. Landseer, for example, had painted the Queen before her marriage. But Winterhalter owed his success to royal patronage after 1842. Most of the Prince's purchases of contemporary works were very orthodox, including such works as *L'Amante* by Augustus Egg and George Cruikshank's *Disturbing the Congregation*. But he did purchase a picture by John Martin, *The Eve of the Deluge*, painted in 1840. He did not, however, patronize Turner, who travelled to Coburg in the autumn of 1840, producing a number of views, including one of the Rosenau, exhibited at the Academy the following year, but firmly ignored by Prince Albert.[3]

The Queen's souvenir albums are full of splendid watercolours recording the royal couple's trips abroad, their houses, their yachts, their official visits to country houses, to Manchester, to Ireland, to open Leeds Town Hall — painted by a small group of artists including Joseph Nash, Eugene Lami for some of the more elaborate balls, John Roberts, G. H. Thomas, who painted many of the military subjects, and W. L. Leitch, one of the Queen's drawing-masters. Artists were employed on specific subjects: John Wilson Carmichael specialized in marine subjects; Frederich Wilhelm Keyl was invited to Windsor to paint the Queen's dogs and the Prince's farm animals, including his pen of prize-winning Windsor pigs. Another animal portrait-painter was Sydney Cooper who has left an account of a visit to Osborne, specifically to paint a favourite Guernsey cow. Cooper was at Osborne several days, and the Prince Albert came over to the farmyard several times to see how the painting was progressing. He stayed to chat with Cooper about the progress of art in the

66 Sir Edwin Landseer (1803–73), photographed in 1860. One of the Royal couple's favourite artists, he was often invited to Balmoral, Osborne and Windsor, giving the Queen and the Prince lessons in drawing, and painting their horses and dogs, themselves and their family.

67 *L'Amante* by
Augustus Egg. An
example of one of the
lighter contemporary
works Prince Albert
purchased. It hung in
his dressing room at
Windsor.

68 *Disturbing the
Congregation* by
George Cruikshank.
Bought by the Prince
in 1850.

69 Franz Xavier Winterhalter (1805–73), in 1854. Court painter to a number of royal families, he painted a very large number of portraits of the Queen and the Prince and their family.

country, informally and pleasantly, showing him over the grounds at Osborne, and explaining his projects for planting and farming.[4] Other artists have left descriptions of visits from the Prince, and it is clear that he was a well-informed and agreeable critic.

Frith, who discussed *Derby Day* with the Prince, paid him a real tribute in speaking of his knowledge of the 'conduct of a picture'.

He told me why I had done certain things and how, if a certain change had been made, my object would have been assisted. How the masses of light and shade might be still more evenly balanced, and how some parts of the picture might receive still more completion. I put many of the Prince's suggestions to the proof after the close of the exhibition, and I improved my picture in every instance.[5]

The Prince seems to have been more adventurous than the Queen in his tastes, since there is evidence that he arranged for Millais's *Christ in the House of His Parents* to be shown to the Queen in 1850, but no purchase was made.[6]

But more important than his patronage of contemporary works was his purchase of early German and early Italian paintings, where his taste was very much ahead of his fellow collectors. As Frank Davis has shown in his study of Victorian collecting, the Prince's taste enriched the National Gallery, as well as the Royal Collections. Among the paintings listed in the posthumous Osborne Catalogue of 1876 were the Duccio *Crucifixion*, bought in 1846, Fra Angelico's *St. Peter Martyr*, Lucas Cranach's *Apollo and Diana*, and *Madonna and Child*, attributed to Verrochio, bought for him by the Queen.[7]

Many of these purchases were made on his behalf by Ludwig Gruner, an art expert from Dresden, who was employed as the Prince's 'adviser on art' from 1843 onwards. He was responsible for buying paintings abroad in both Germany and Italy, and he helped with advice in the decoration of apartments in the royal palaces, particularly at Osborne and Buckingham Palace. He was responsible for publishing the book on the experiment with frescoes in the Buckingham Palace Pavilion, a field in which his knowledge of chromolithography was extremely useful.

The Prince was not only a collector, he was by nature a cataloguer and a classifier. Early in his married life he set in hand the cataloguing, and in some cases the re-hanging, of the existing royal collections. There was a great need for reform here as elsewhere in the royal establishment. Mrs. Jameson, who later wrote the guide to the Buckingham Palace Pavilion, wrote in 1842:

Something I have ventured to say of the disgraceful state of the Royal Galleries at Windsor and Hampton Court, but not a hundredth part of what I felt and thought, and have heard expressed by others . . . One

official stands in another's way and there is a sort of terror of all interference or suggestion which I do not understand. Perhaps the little I
have to say may excite the attention of those who have the power, as I
believe they have the will, to amend a state of affairs worthy of the most
Gothic ignorance and barbarism.[8]

The following year the Prince seems to have taken the hang-
ing and the distribution of the royal pictures in hand, not only at
Windsor and Hampton Court, but also at Buckingham Palace,
and Frogmore House, occupied by the Duchess of Kent.[9] In due
course the cataloguing was put into Redgrave's competent
hands, a task which he completed only in 1876, 15 years after
the Prince's death.

Prince Albert was also active in other, less public, areas of the
royal collections. He and the Queen started an enamels collec-

ALBERTVS.PRINC.CONS. RESTAVR.A.S.MDCCCLX

Top, left
72 The Prince's bust above the door in the Print Room at Windsor Castle.

Bottom, left
73 *Undine* by Daniel Maclise. Engraved in 1855 for the *Art Journal* which published a number of works from the Royal collections.

tion, which was to include portraits of the whole English royal family.[10] There were also collections made of portraits of the French royal families, and one of the whole Coburg cousinage, which were made up of copies of miniatures from those families' collections.

In December 1842, he had turned his attention to the Print Collection, again arranging for its classification. For it, he fitted up the Print Room at Windsor Castle, under William IV's Library, and within the Carolean wing overlooking Eton. It is a charming Jacobean apartment, decorated with a scholarly plaster ceiling, with the Prince's head set within a roundel. Here he and the Queen would withdraw to look at their collections of engravings and prints. This was not only a tidying up of what they contained but a positive and successful attempt to build up a collection of fine contemporary engravings. For instance, when, in due course, the *Art Journal* published engravings of treasures from the royal collections, copies of the engravings in three different states were supplied to the Library, as well as two sets of the completed engravings for which the Prince and the Queen subscribed.[11]

The Prince's true dimensions as an art historian manqué are revealed, however, by the work he put in hand on the study of Raphael. This was intended to be the first of several such studies, Michelangelo being another artist already identified by the Prince as suitable for such treatment. The intention was to create a *corpus* of comparative material on Raphael — that is, all the prints and engravings already published, together with photographs of all other Raphael or attributed Raphael works then known. The Raphael works in the royal collections themselves were also photographed. Some 1,500 items were collected by the time that the catalogue was published, and this mass of material has been deposited in the British Museum for the use of scholars. The Prince's librarian, Dr. Becker, started the work, and he was succeeded by Herr Ruland, who later went on to become Director of the Grand Ducal Museum of Saxe-Weimar.

The whole scheme has breadth and imagination as well as revealing an interest in order and intellectual organization, in the use of an existing collection to aid scholars. The interchange of information between libraries, together with the gathering in of all kinds of reproductions from engravings to newly available photographs and chromolithographs, make it a prototype for the sort of scholarly project so gladly espoused by modern American foundations. There were clearly occasional repercussions since scholarly research can reveal misattributions as well as lost masterpieces. At least one owner attacked the Prince for alleged prejudice against a Raphael which he owned, complaining that he had been denied access to foreign collections through the

74 Dr. Carl Ruland, Librarian to Prince Albert, in 1860. He completed the great work on Raphael after the Prince's death.

machinations of the Prince and his agents.[12]

An indirect result of this study was the moving of the Raphael Cartoons for the Mortlake Tapestries from Hampton Court to the new South Kensington Museum. This was not done until after the Prince's death, but the Queen gave permission, knowing how interested the Prince had been in both the Cartoons and the Museum. The operation was achieved in typical South Kensington fashion. Francis Fowke designed a special wagon in which the Cartoons could be transported safely within the day. Once installed, the Cartoons were photographed by the resident sapper photographers with a specially designed camera.

The Prince's interest in Raphael is shown in the way in which several buildings are decorated with copies of Raphael works, including the Ballroom at Buckingham Palace and the Frogmore Mausoleum.

The Prince had wanted to remove the National Gallery and its precious collections away from the dangerous pollution of Trafalgar Square to the purer region of South Kensington. He does not seem to have been the originator of the idea, but he espoused it wholeheartedly. The South Kensington Museum made a special study of pollution, proving that even their gaslit rooms were superior atmospherically to rooms in central London. Despite 'London particulars' (heavy smoke, dirty streets littered with horse manure, foul effluvia from the Thames, all before air conditioning) there was a strong lobby to retain the pictures in central London. 'H.R.H. F.M. P.A. at it again,' growled *Punch*. And, in the event, inertia or vested interests carried the day: the Royal Academy moved to Burlington House; the pictures have stayed in Trafalgar Square.

The Prince's influence on the National Gallery was, however, very considerable through his close relations with Charles Eastlake who, according to one authority, 'abandoned a promising career as a third-rate painter to become the foremost – indeed the only – English picture expert of the mid-century. He was marvellously gifted for what was a new profession – scholarly, sensitive, industrious, with a sense of humour and blessed with a no less gifted partner in his wife, Elizabeth Rigby.'[13]

In due course, the establishment of South Kensington and the Museum headed by Henry Cole was to give the Prince another sphere of influence in the art world. It, too, was to build up a splendid picture collection through such acquisitions as the Sheepshanks Collection of works by contemporary artists, the Vernon Collection, and even such temporary residents as the Turner Collection.

As an executant, the Prince was a competent amateur, with a real gift for caricature shown by his early sketches. Lady East-

NATIONAL GALLERY.

H. R. H. F. M. P. A. AT IT AGAIN!

Policeman. "ONLY MOVING THE PICTURES TO KENSINGTON GORE! SUPPOSE YOU LEAVE 'EM WHERE THEY ARE, EH?"

75 *H.R.H. F.M. P.A. at it again! Punch,* July 12, 1856, opposed the scheme to move the national collections from the National Gallery in Trafalgar Square to salubrious South Kensington.

lake saw the man in the artist, 'he may be truly said to have handled even a pencil consistently with the nature of his mind. His slightest design, his most hasty suggestion on paper, bore on it the character of a beginning and an end – the sense of a whole – to which few amateurs attain.'[14]

The Prince himself did not claim more than a working knowledge. As he observed to Lady Bloomfield at dinner at Windsor:

I consider that persons in our position of life can never be distinguished artists . . . Our business is not so much to create, as to learn to appreciate and understand the works of others, and we never do this till we have realised the difficulties to be overcome. Acting on this principle myself, I have always tried to learn the rudiments of art as much as possible. For instance, I learnt oil-painting, watercolours, etching, lithography etc. etc., and in music I learnt thorough bass, the pianoforte, organ, and singing, – not of course, with a view of doing anything worth looking at or hearing, but simply to enable me to judge and appreciate the works of others.[15]

76 The Queen's terrier Islay drawn and engraved by Landseer.

Opposite page
77 Islay drawn by Queen Victoria and etched by Prince Albert.

Edwin Landseer and his brother called at Windsor on July 2, 1842, to show the royal couple how to etch, demonstrating by etching a portrait of Islay begging.

In fact, the Prince seems to have enjoyed drawing and sketching with the Queen in the early years of their married life. This was obviously so well known that it was the subject of at least one caricature. The royal couple also learnt to etch, on one occasion summoning Edwin Landseer and his brother, Tom, to Buckingham Palace to instruct them. Edwin Landseer etched his own sketch of Islay begging, a rather more lively portrait than that by the Prince. However, the Queen and the Prince produced at least one charming joint portrait of their children.[16]

'In feeling for the sister art,' wrote Lady Eastlake in her obituary of the Prince,' he was — and, we are inclined to think, in this only — true to the German type of race. He loved music with all a German's heart.' She went on to praise his influence on the music chosen for public occasions such as the Duke of Wellington's funeral, concluding however, that 'the taste which presided over the programme of Her Majesty's exquisite concerts was only too cultivated for the majority of the favoured listeners.'[17]

A modern critic has endorsed this view of the Prince's tastes as avant-garde at least as far as the aristocracy went. Professional musical taste he points out was 'already all but overwhelmed' by German music, and the Prince's introduction of works by Schubert, Beethoven and Mozart had less effect here.[18]

The Prince was able to exercise his musical taste in three main areas. First of all, he reorganized the Queen's private band of wind instruments into a full orchestra, a reform which fitted in well with his other Household changes. He made it more effective, and gave it more demanding and varied programmes. This was one of his more immediate changes and the enlarged band first played on December 24, 1840. In addition, he had new organs installed at both Windsor Castle, and in the fine new Ball Room at Buckingham Palace.

His second musical platform was the Concerts of Antient Music, an existing society to whom 'ancient' meant music over a quarter of a century old. He presided over his first concert in April 1840, and seems to have arranged the programme for one or two concerts a year thereafter. These always contained a majority of 'new' material including works by Palestrina and other renaissance composers, lesser known works by Mozart, Handel and Beethoven, scenes from Gluck operas, and even medieval chorales and a *Romance provencale* by Thibault, King of Navarre.

The Concerts of Antient Music finally collapsed in 1848, and possibly the Prince would have had less time for such projects in any case, though he did manage to choose music for the concerts of the Philharmonic Society until 1860. These concerts were conducted by different people, including both Mendelssohn

ISLAY

VR. del.ᵗ   ¹¹/₉ 1840.   Albert. sc.ᵗ

and Wagner on a visit[19] in 1855 when the programme included the Overture to *Tannhauser*.

Of his own compositions, musical critics do not hold an exaggeratedly high opinion. He published a number of works, some with his brother before he came to England, and in the 1880s a collected edition was issued. Lady Lyttelton has left a description of the Queen calling her attention to the Prince's 'piece of solemn choral music' played at dinner by the 1st Life Guards band; but perhaps little of his music would have been performed without his high position.[20] Nonetheless, he brought the musical traditions and talents of the Coburg family into prominence; both his compositions and those of the Duchess of Kent were performed at Court; he made German music fashionable in the highest circles, and perhaps made life more agreeable for visiting musicians.[21]

Weber, on his ill-fated trip to England in 1826, had found that musicians – even composers – were treated like upper servants; Mendelssohn in 1842 found a very different reception from the Queen and the Prince. He has left a charming picture of an interview with them at Buckingham Palace, the royal couple joining in and singing to his piano-playing, the Prince playing a 'Chorale, by heart, with the pedals, so charmingly, clearly and correctly, that it would have done credit to any professional . . .', and then all the music sheets going all over the floor, and being picked up by the Queen . . .[22]

78 Westminster Hall in July 1843, filled with the entries for the fresco competition. 140 were received, and proved a popular public attraction.

CHAPTER SIX

The First Royal Commission: Decorating the Houses of Parliament

CUPID OUT OF PLACE.

79 *Cupid out of Place. Punch*'s comment on the Prince's lack of employment. The word 'cartoon' replaced 'pencilling' in *Punch*'s vocabulary after 1843, and acquired the meaning of satirical sketch.

It was Sir Robert Peel who suggested that Prince Albert should take the chair of the Royal Commission appointed to select the works of art to adorn the new Palace of Westminster.

When the old Palace had been burnt down in 1834, the opportunity to build anew was seized eagerly. *The Times* had called for the 'erection of a noble Parliamentary edifice worthy of a great nation'; the legislators were to have a building with 'space, form, facility of hearing, facility of ventilation, facility of access, and amplitude of accommodation for *the public* as well as for the members themselves, and for those who have immediate business with them'.[1] To all this was to be added artistic excellence: 'The building will be regarded as part and parcel of the intellect of the age, as the model par excelence (*sic*), the example in character, art and decoration, of what is to come after.'[2]

Sir Charles Barry had been appointed to design the building in 1836, but it was not till 1841 that a select committee was appointed to consider the 'promotion of the fine arts of this country in connection with the rebuilding of the Houses of Parliament'. The select committee included Sir Robert Peel, not yet Prime Minister, the President of the Board of Trade, Sir Henry Labouchere (1798–1869), and a group of members considered to be informed and interested in matters of art.[3]

Their terms of reference were somewhat obscure and, after hearing a certain number of witnesses, they came to the conclusion that a Royal Commission should be set up to deal with the question of decorating the new building.

The new Commission was set up in the autumn of 1841, by Sir Robert Peel who had just succeeded Lord Melbourne as Prime Minister. He shared an interest in art with the Prince who visited his house in Whitehall Gardens to see his collection of pictures, and he turned to the Prince very early in the project to ask him to head the Commission. The Prince made two stipulations, one was his invariable veto on party distinction, and the other was that no professional artists would be included as members of the Commission. He felt that their opinions would be 'even better obtained by taking it upon examination, as this would enable the Commission to procure the different opinions of a greater number of artists'. He also felt the presence of artists might inhibit laymen in discussing artistic matters.[4] In October Peel could announce to the House of Commons that the Prince would be Chairman of the Commission, and within a fortnight the list of Commissioners had been announced.

The Royal Commission was similar in make-up to the select committee. In the bitter words of Richard Redgrave, a partisan of the Prince, but no sycophant, he was:

surrounded by the most eminent statesmen of all parties, with some representatives of the literature and dilettantism of the country: art was strangely omitted, except by the appointment of Mr. Eastlake as secretary. The commission was in fact, admirably constituted for the determination of the most abstract questions of State policy, rather than to descend to technical art matters, such as the relative merits of oil or fresco, the most fitting subjects . . .[5]

The Prince revelled in the new opportunity: '. . . these sittings (besides the interest in the subject itself) give me an agreeable opportunity, which otherwise I should not have, to get more intimately acquainted with some of the most distinguished men of the day without reference to politics.'[6]

The Royal Commission, though appointed to consider the decorating of the new palace in terms of the fine arts, both in terms of the 'beneficial and elevating effect of the fine arts upon a people' and in the prosaic results of that patronage 'in creating new objects of industry and enjoyment' and therefore stimulating trade and manufacture, found itself somewhat restricted. Barry had already completed his plans and designs, and managed early in the Commission's life to establish that they would be responsible for large decorative paintings, but only for freestanding sculpture not 'architectonic or conventional sculpture that will be required to adorn the several elevations'.[7] It was already established that fresco painting would be the most suit-

80 *Neptune resigning the Empire of the Sea to Britannia* by William Dyce (1806–64). A sketch for the large fresco on the main staircase at Osborne. Dyce was one of the few artists working in England who could manage true fresco.

81 Wallpainting by J. Schnorr von
Carolsfeld, in the Residenz at Munich,
depicting the death of Siegfried from the
Nibelungenlied.

able medium for the decoration of large areas, though some oil
paintings would be needed.

The earlier select committee had heard evidence from William
Dyce, Director of the new Government School of Design at
Somerset House, and other experts on the suitability of fresco
painting for the adornment of large areas, and for expertise on
true fresco painting at the period it was necessary to turn to
Germany. Dyce had studied in Germany, and, in the autumn of
1841, Peter von Cornelius came to London and met Sir Robert
Peel. Cornelius had been working in Munich for Ludwig I of
Bavaria, and was later to work in Berlin. Ludwig I had already
commissioned a great series of frescoes from J. Schnorr von
Carolsfeld on the theme of the Niebelunglied to decorate the
Residenz in Munich, and there were other German artists of the
Nazarene school working in Italy. For this reason, Eastlake was
apprehensive that Prince Albert would advocate the employment, not only of German technicians expert in fresco painting,
but also of German artists, but the Prince told him that he
thought that English artists could easily learn the technique.

The Commission presented its first report in April 1842, together with the announcement of a competition for cartoon drawings 'executed in chalk or charcoal, not less than ten or more than fifteen feet in their longest dimension; . . . illustrating subjects from British History or from the works of Spenser, Shakespeare or Milton', to be presented the following year.[8]

In his first meeting with Eastlake, the Prince had discussed the encouragement of a school of fresco painting, one of the objectives of the original select committee of 1835, who had wanted to find employment for the young artists being trained by the School of Design.

There are two great auxiliaries in this country which seldom fail to promote the success of any scheme, – fashion and a high example. Fashion, we know, is all in all in England, and if the Court – I mean the Queen and myself – set the example hereafter . . . the same taste will extend itself to wealthy individuals.'[9]

In 1843, he put this belief into practice, commissioning a whole series of fresco decorations for a cottage in the Buckingham Palace garden. This was decorated after the manner of a garden pavilion in Rome, in a variety of styles, employing some of the artists who had entered the national competition, inspired by some of the same themes.

The three rooms of the cottage, each decorated to a different theme, survive only in the chromolithographs published by Ludwig Gruner. They certainly give the impression of a brighter and more successful application of the fresco technique than that achieved later at the Houses of Parliament, possibly because of the smaller scale.

One room was decorated throughout in the Pompeian manner by Augustine Aglio, an Italian artist who had worked at Drury Lane Theatre and the Italianate Roman Catholic Cathedral in Moorfields. One romantic room was based on the Waverley Novels of Scott, and the important central room on *Comus* by John Milton. Here Dyce, Maclise and Eastlake were employed from the Parliamentary competitors, and the Prince added two favourite royal artists – Sir William Ross, painter of the Queen's favourite miniature of the Prince, and Edwin Landseer – as well as Clarkson and Thomas Uwins.

The royal couple took a great personal interest in the work, and Uwins wrote to a friend in August 1843:

Coming to us twice a day unannounced, and without attendants, entirely stript of all state and ceremony, courting conversation, and desiring reason rather than obedience, they have gained our admiration and love.

In many things they are an example to the age. They have breakfasted, heard morning prayers with the household in the private Chapel, and are out some distance from the Palace talking to us in the summer-

82 The Scott Room in the Pavilion.

house, before half-past nine o'clock – sometimes earlier. After the public duties of the day, and before their dinner, they come out again, evidently delighted to get away from the bustle of the world to enjoy each other's society in the solitude of the garden.[10]

Work on the cottage began in June 1843, in the same month that the cartoons for the Parliamentary competition were assembled for exhibition to the public. Again the Prince took a personal interest, visiting Westminster Hall to see them unpacked.[11]

The resulting 140 cartoons were exhibited to the public in July 1843 in Westminster Hall. Eastlake noted with interest that though he had

abridged the Catalogue to a penny size for the million, . . . many of the most wretchedly dressed people prefer the sixpenny one with the quotations, and it is a very gratifying sight to witness the . . . earnestness with which they follow the subject with the books in their hands . . . these Catalogues in the hands of so many thousands would be the first introduction . . . to our best poets and writers . . .[12]

86

The artists concentrated on the earlier episodes in English history, many chosen from before the Norman Conquest, the first prize going to Edward Armitage's *Caesar's Invasion of Britain*, the second to G. F. Watts for *Caractacus Led in Triumph through the Streets of Rome*, and C. W. Cope taking the third for the *First Trial by Jury*. The prize-winning entries were widely published in lithographs, thus ensuring their survival, since most of the original cartoons have perished.

The Commission then arranged a further competition, this time to test the capacity of the various artists to paint in the fresco manner, and only placed the first real commission in 1845 when Dyce was assigned *The Baptism of Ethelbert*. He promptly went off to the continent to improve his fresco technique, returning the following year with yet another report. Maclise, Cope and J. C. Horsley were commissioned the following year, and other smaller commissions were also placed.

By 1848, the first four frescoes were visible to the public, and Maclise was commissioned to paint the *Spirit of Justice*, as a companion to his *Spirit of Chivalry*, and Cope *Prince Henry acknowledging the Authority of Justice Gascoigne*. However, there was a growing dissatisfaction with true fresco, where the artist paints on wet plaster which is fresh every day. The artists later turned to the waterglass technique by which the subject was painted on a dry wall in watercolour and then sprayed with waterglass to fix it. This was a German technique advocated by Prince Albert, and has in fact proved more resistant to the London atmosphere than true fresco. Dyce's two great paintings in the Royal Gallery were carried out in this medium, and indeed he was only prepared to execute them in this manner. The Prince's last contribution to the work of the Commission was to persuade Maclise to paint his *Meeting of Wellington and Blücher* and his *Death of Nelson*, partly through his advocacy of the waterglass technique, and partly by promising to eliminate the stained glass which Maclise thought would destroy the effect of his paintings.[13]

The Commissioners also concerned themselves with sculpture, though again their dilatoriness militated against the filling of the corridors and halls with any great speed. A number of oil paintings were commissioned, and these were on the whole more successful because the technique was better understood by the English artists, the size usually more manageable, and the medium less easily damaged by the London atmosphere.

By the end of the 1840s the Royal Fine Art Commission was losing its impetus. It was not only in *Punch* that there were complaints of dilatoriness: the House of Commons was restive, and Barry had solved the problem of the other decorative work such as ironwork, ceramic tiles and so forth by treating it all as part of the architecture and putting it in hand without reference to

83 Detail of cartoon for the Meeting of Blucher and Wellington by Daniel Maclise, who was only persuaded to undertake the work by the personal intervention of the Prince Consort himself. The painting of the fresco was not completed until March 1862.

the Commissioners. Prince Albert was gradually being diverted to more serious matters of state; his ally Peel died in 1850, and Eastlake went on to become first President of the Royal Academy, and then Director of the National Gallery. The story of the decoration of the Palace of Westminster did not end until long after the Prince's death, and has been admirably and fully told by T. S. R. Boase.

As he points out, far from encouraging the development of new forms in art, the project fell far short of the high aspirations. Many young painters were impeded in their careers by the high expectations aroused by the Commission, coupled with the practical meanness of the rewards actually distributed to the artists. All the difficulties of 'aesthetic planning by a committee and of divided control between Commission and architect' compounded the problems attached to any Parliamentary project.

While the Great Exhibition convinced the country that the arts could be practically applied, they had the humiliating experience of seeing their own frescoes perishing through technical incompetence. The hopes of High Art ended in disappointment and a botched-up conclusion. Historical painting was discredited rather than established . . .[14]

How much the 'submerged conflict between the English and German traditions' that he particularly blames for Dyce's failures is Prince Albert's fault is not clear. It must be said in Prince Albert's defence that it was the 1835 Select Committee which decided to use fresco and, though the Prince used this technique for two works commissioned by him, once its shortcomings were known, he became as keen an advocate of the more successful waterglass technique. It is to him indeed that we owe the finest paintings in the Palace of Westminster, the two heroic Maclises.

Richard Redgrave concluded bitterly in 1866:

The sole object really entrusted to the commission by Her Majesty was the *inquiry* how the fine arts of the country might be encouraged and promoted. But the Commission proceeded to attempt to carry out the plans they recommended; and the attempt proved disastrous. . . . So far from art having been encouraged and promoted, we fear it has been checked and discouraged; that young men were allured from their own walks in art, tempted into hopeless competitions, . . . and then left sick at heart, with diminished means . . .[15]

For the young man in charge, Prince Albert, it was an initiation into the peculiar ways of British democracy. It demonstrates, through his choice of Eastlake, his ability to choose and inspire able assistants; the decision so attacked by Redgrave to bar all artists from the Commission was his, possibly also the attempt to carry out the Commission's recommendations rather than merely to advise. On the other hand, his own private commission was rapidly undertaken and rapidly completed, suggesting that the problem was that of designing by committee. He doubtless learnt too how to manage an English committee, experience that stood him in good stead when he came to the second Royal Commission — that for the Exhibition of 1851.

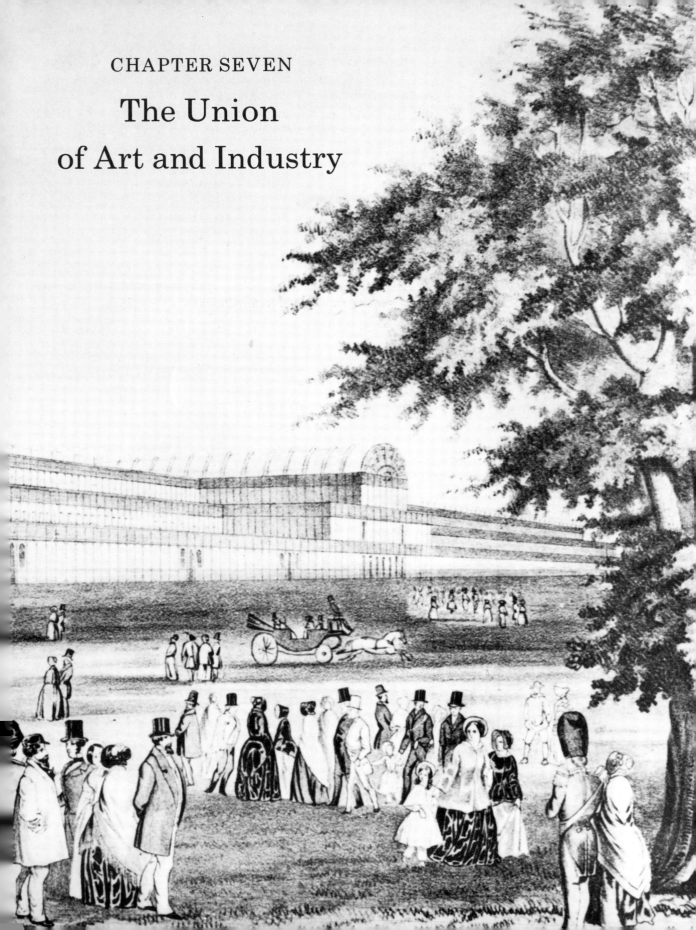

CHAPTER SEVEN

The Union
of Art and Industry

Prince Albert joined the Society of Arts very soon after his arrival in England, and became its President in 1843. It was one of the first organizations in which he played an active part: his role in the revival of what had become a moribund body was critical. Through the Society, he came into touch with many of the most important of the satellite figures with whom he shared an enthusiasm for the arts, and particularly for the arts in an industrial context.

The Society of Arts was founded in 1754 'for the Encouragement of Arts, Manufacturers and Commerce' – in an appropriately contemporary manner in a Covent Garden coffee house. Its worthy aims were to be pursued through the giving of prizes for the discovery of useful substances or the invention of useful appliances or machines. Other prizes were given for proficiency in drawing or accurate surveys. The prize money came from the members' subscriptions. In the first 25 years of its existence the Society expended some £16,625 in premiums, and these went to a very wide range of inventions, helpful in the fields of architecture and design, and even more directed towards the improvement of agriculture and industry. Colonial projects and cultivations were encouraged as domestic manufactures. The prize-winning appliances make a fascinating list. Drill-ploughs, root-slicers and chaff cutters were symbols of the Agricultural Revolution which created so much of the prosperity which enabled England to stand alone against Napoleon. Looms, cranes and pumps were of equal use to the growing host of mechanized industries which created the new towns of the Midlands and the north-west. Life-saving devices were not neglected: among the inventors rewarded were John Davies for his extending ladder for escaping from fire; John Robert for his respirator; and Greathead lifeboat, together with a lighted buoy, which could be thrown to seafarers who had fallen overboard, and 'a mortar apparatus' for throwing a line to a stranded ship. Artists and sculptors were also honoured: Flaxman and Nollekens, Lawrence and Landseer were all recognized in their time. It was in the Society's rooms that the first art exhibition of works of art by contemporary artists was held – in 1760 – some nine years before the founding of the Royal Academy.

However, the Society's initial successes were followed by a period of decline. By the 1830s this was becoming very serious, and the Society was clearly flagging in the matter of both finances and influence. This was partly due to its very success: the pioneering efforts in the field of manufactures had been succeeded by commercial rewards which made the Society's prizes seem small. Equally the artists who had organized the first exhibition had been inspired by its success to found their own societies. New, specialized institutions were competing for both enthusiasm and money, while all these developments were taking place against the background of the severe post-war slump.

This was the declining institution which the newly arrived Prince Albert joined in June 1843. The royal connection was strong: the Duke of Sussex, one of the younger sons of George III, had been the President since 1816, and he took an early opportunity of introducing Prince Albert. On the Duke's death in 1843, the Prince succeeded him. 'From the moment that he assumed the presidency,' writes one of the Society's historians, 'he impressed on the Society that the main object of its existence henceforth must be the application of science and art to industrial purposes; and the Society soon learned that it could expect from him, not merely a formal consideration of routine matters, but a quick and wise judgement on any important question that was submitted for his opinion.'[1]

He was fortunate that at this time the Society attracted — possibly because of his leadership — a number of outstanding members. The man with whom he was to have most dealings was Henry Cole, but others concerned with the Society during his Presidency included Dr. Lyon Playfair, the chemist, already known to the Prince through his report on the kitchens at Buckingham Palace; Richard Redgrave, the artist; Robert Stephenson, the engineer; Joseph Paxton, at this time still best known as gardener to the bachelor Duke of Devonshire; Joseph Hume, the radical M.P.; and C. Wentworth Dilke. The Secretary from 1845 onwards was John Scott Russell, F.R.S., a naval architect who designed the Great Eastern steamship.

Henry Cole (1808–1882) became one of the Prince's most important colleagues, first in the work which culminated in the Great Exhibition of 1851, and then in the creation of the South Kensington complex, and particularly that for the Museum which grew into the V. & A.

Cole developed idiosyncrasies which made him an easily caricatured figure, with his mane of hair, his inevitable little dog scuttling after him down the South Kensington corridors, and his unenviable reputation for riding roughshod to get his own way. In later life, Lord Derby once referred to him as 'the most generally unpopular man I know'. For the Prince he was an invaluable ally — the Queen recalled how he used to say 'We must have steam, get Cole' — and without such a man, full of sympathetic ideas, of a similar energy and dynamism, always ready to execute schemes, the Prince would have found his South Kensington project impossible.

Prince Albert first came across Cole in 1842 when the latter was working for the Record Commission, cataloguing and transcribing the State Records. Cole's system of classification had

85 *Men of the Day, No. 29:* 'King Cole'. Henry Cole with his little dog from a *Vanity Fair* cartoon of 1871.

intrigued the Prince, whose own papers were impeccably filed at Windsor, often titled in his own hand. However, Henry Cole was very much more than a clerk – he had been responsible for much of the agitation which had kept the work of the Record Commission going when it was threatened by official apathy and malpractice.[2]

The Society, faced with virtual bankruptcy, in the early 1840s changed its constitution, giving more control to a single Council, instead of many committees, but it needed not only a new framework but a new role. In 1844 the Secretary, Francis Whishaw, revived the idea of an exhibition, a Grand Annual Exhibition of Manufactures – a form of activity which the Society had adopted in the early years but which had fallen into disuse. On the continent, however, the idea of national government-sponsored exhibitions was gaining ground. Both the French government, and the newly formed Zollverein or Customs Union of North German States dominated by Prussia, held exhibitions in 1844. Whishaw tried out two small, one day 'exhibitions' of machinery and pictures on the Society's premises, and this aroused enough support to lead to a proposal for 'periodical Exhibitions of Works of Industry, at which the producers shall be invited to display their various productions'.[3]

In view of the way in which this project developed it is worth looking at the resolution adopted by the Society's steering committee in May 1845:

That the experience of foreign countries has proved that great national advantages have been derived from the stimulus given to industrial skill by bringing the manufactures of different establishments into competition with each other, and by presenting Honorary rewards to those who have excelled in each department, cheapness of production and excellence of material, both in execution and durability, being assumed as the criteria of superiority.[4]

The committee went on to conclude that it was the 'peculiar province' of the Society to promote 'such a periodical Exhibition of Works of Industry'. It seems to have been an idiosyncratic British assumption that such exhibitions, which were organized in France and elsewhere by the government, could be successfully promoted by a voluntary society.

Whishaw took the opportunity of putting the idea to Prince Albert when he came to present the Society's annual prizes. The Prince listened, and asked that, when the 'plan for carrying it into effect should be matured', it should be laid before him. This took place in 1845, and disposes of the claim made by Theodore Martin, the Prince's official biographer, that the idea of an Exhibition had originated with the Prince.[5] Nonetheless, he was sympathetic to the idea, and it seems likely that it would not

86 The 'Felix Summerley' Tea Service designed by Cole in 1845.

have received official endorsement without the backing of a man of the Prince's standing. In the England of the 1840s, a wealthy peer of an inventive turn of mind or with industrial enthusiasms could have achieved the same result. Such men were found in the realm of the arts or architecture, such as the Earl of Ellesmere or Earl de Grey, or Lord Shaftesbury in the field of philanthropy; but the English aristocracy at this period was not immediately involved in industry nor very educated in science. The Prince, with his ready interest in education and his understanding of technical matters, was uniquely qualified to promote such an idea.

John Scott Russell, an able but brusque Scot, became Secretary of the Society in the autumn of 1845, and he appears to have persuaded Henry Cole, already a colleague, together with Wentworth Dilke, on the *Railway Chronicle*, to take an interest in the Society and its proposed Exhibitions. Together they drummed up support, first for the Society's competitions, then for the exhibitions and finally for the Society's proposed 'Grand Annual Exhibition of Manufactures'.

Cole had already tried his hand at promoting artistic objects, the most memorable of which was the first Christmas card ever published for sale. It was drawn for Cole by J. C. Horsley, and sold for the Christmas trade in 1843. It was sold as the 'Felix Summerley Christmas Card', a nom-de-plume Cole had invented for his *Home Treasury* and for some guide book pamphlets. In 1845 he designed a Felix Summerley tea-set, which was made by Minton's and submitted to the first Society of Arts competition. It was so successful that it was followed by a number of other 'Art Manufactures' some of which were bought by Prince Albert.

From 1846 onwards the Society, led by John Scott Russell as Secretary, promoted a series of annual competitions, chiefly to generate interest in the idea of a national exhibition. The first competition attracted little and rather amateurish support; perhaps the most significant thing about it was the Felix Summerley Art Manufactures. The second provided enough entries of standing for an exhibition, though these had to be supplemented by articles begged from manufacturers. Leading manufacturers

EXTERIOR OF THE BIRMINGHAM EXPOSITION BUILDING.

gradually became aware of the value of exhibiting their products, and by 1848 the idea was a success. That year the exhibition attracted over 700 exhibits, and some 70,000 visitors thronged the Society's premises. In 1849, the restricted and specialized exhibits included the centrepiece designed by Prince Albert and lent by the Queen.

The credit for the international character of the Great Exhibition is difficult to apportion: as always in successful cases, it is claimed by all the parties concerned – or their supporters. At the time of the famous meeting of June 30, 1849, at which the main lines of the 1851 Exhibition were 'settled', two Exhibitions were in everyone's minds. The first was the Birmingham Exhibition held in a temporary building for which in fact foreign exhibits were invited but not received, and the second was the current French national Exhibition, which M. Buffet, the French Minister of Agriculture and Commerce, had wanted to make international.[6] It was perhaps difficult to resist the feeling that the Society's proposed exhibition would have to be international to achieve a 'first'.

There is an intriguing 'kitchen Cabinet' story which throws light on men surrounding the Prince. Digby Wyatt, Henry Cole and Francis Fuller, also a member of the Society of Arts committee working on the exhibition, all went to Paris to see the Exhibition. Francis Fuller, returning alone on June 12, found himself travelling from Southampton with Thomas Cubitt, the London builder, who had been to Osborne House, in the Isle of Wight, where he was working for the Prince. They naturally discussed the Paris Exhibition, and Fuller recorded in his diary: 'I informed him that we could do a much grander work in London by inviting contributions from every nation; and said, moreover, that if Prince Albert would take the lead in such a work he would become a leading light among nations.'[7] Cubitt relayed this to Prince Albert.

Two days later, the Prince gave the prizes for the Society and Scott Russell took the opportunity to refer publicly to a 'large national exhibition of specimens of Manufactures and Arts taking place in 1851'. Scott Russell was summoned to Buckingham Palace on June 20 to discuss the statement, and a meeting was called for ten days later. Cole took the opportunity to call on the 29th, and to discuss matters with the Prince. Cole recorded in his autobiography:

At the moment the Prince came into the room and entered fully into the ideas of the Exhibition so far as they had been developed. He thought the Exhibition should be a large one and suggested that a permanent building might be erected in Leicester Square . . . I observed that there appeared to me to be an earlier question than the site, and I asked if he considered the Exhibition should be a National or International Exhibition . . . The Prince reflected for a minute and then said, 'It must embrace foreign productions,' to use his words, and added emphatically, 'International, certainly.' Upon which I said, 'Do you think, sir, Leicester Square, would be large enough?' He replied, 'Certainly not, for works of all nations. Where do you think it should be?' I answered, 'In Hyde Park.'[8]

Those present at the meeting on June 30 were the Prince himself, Cole, Scott Russell, Fuller and, unusually, Thomas Cubitt who probably attended at the Prince's express request because of his building experience.

The minutes remain in the possession of the Society, with manuscript corrections in the Prince Consort's hand. At that meeting the main objectives of the Great Exhibition were settled. Most important was the matter of the scope of the Exhibition, and this minute was almost wholly drafted by the Prince:

It was a question of whether this Exhibition should be exclusively limited to British Industry. It was considered that, whilst it appears an error to fix any limitation to the production of Machinery, Science and Taste, which are of no country, but belong, as a whole, to the civilised world, particular advantage to British Industry might be derived from placing it in fair competition with that of other nations.[9]

There is an interesting Free Trade note about the advantages to British Industry of feeling the winds of competition, which may seem as dated as the equally insistent contemporary idea that more Exhibitions would increase the chances of peace, and that more tourism would lead different races to greater mutual liking and respect. The British manufacturer at the period was not as concerned over foreign competition as the British landowners had been at the passing of the Act repealing the Corn Laws. But there was growing concern over technical education, and one of Prince Albert's objectives after the success of the

89 The Albert Medal, instituted in 1863 by the Royal Society of Arts, in memory of the Prince Consort.

90 Granville George Leveson-Gower, 2nd Earl Granville (1815–91). Whig statesman and a constant ally of the Prince.

Exhibition was to organize better technical education at a poly-technic level for application of art to industry and vice versa.

The June meeting at Buckingham Palace was followed by a further meeting at Osborne, where the President of the Board of Trade, Henry Labouchere, was present. A formal application to the government for the issue of a Royal Commission was made at the end of the month. Then, as now, August was a dead month for official action, so the three members from the Society, Cole, Scott Russell and Fuller, now joined by Digby Wyatt, the archi-tect, sounded out the 'manufacturing districts' in England, Scot-land and Ireland, and even Germany. The Prince was extremely cautious about being seen to espouse any cause, or to use his position to initiate action. His secretary, Phipps, was concerned at Cole's flattering references at a Dublin meeting to the decision to throw the Exhibition 'open to manufacturers of the whole world' being a 'spontaneous act, irrespective of extra influences' by the Prince. It was perhaps the aristocrat in Phipps which led him to caution the Prince against allowing premature public meetings, 'A meeting,' he added, 'in a private room of some of the leading manufacturers and practical men of science, for the purposes of ample discussion, is of course a different thing.'[10]

The agitation for the creation of a Royal Commission con-tinued throughout the autumn and winter of 1849 with the Prince keeping well in the background, until he was certain he had public support and official government approval. With the issue of the Royal Commission (January 3, 1850) the Prince's role became that of the Chairman of a government body not the President of a learned society.

The Prince continued until his death as President of the Society of Arts, seeing its membership rise in his Presidency from 685 to 1,700. He took part in the Society's educational work, instituting a 25 guinea prize for the most successful candidate in the Society's technical exams, something that the Queen carried on after his death. No project of the dramatic importance of the 1851 Exhibition again concerned the Society though, in due course, members of the Society were responsible for running the 1862 Exhibition. The Society through its leading members was con-cerned in the development of the South Kensington site until the end of the 1880s.

The Society honoured its President in two ways. In 1857, they brought out a volume of his speeches, a sincere tribute to the living man, only too rarely paid. They also instituted the Albert Medal in 1863, as the Society's highest honour 'for dis-tinguished merit in Promoting Arts, Manufacture and Com-merce'.

Prince Albert was Chairman of the Royal Commission, a number of leading government figures and others from the fields of the arts and industry were Commissioners, while an Executive Committee included Wentworth Dilke, Cole and Scott Russell. Of the government Ministers, perhaps the most important was Earl Granville (1815–1891), then Vice-President of the Board of Trade. He was an extremely rich and well-connected politician (cousin of the diarist Greville, known as the 'Lodger' because he lived with the Granvilles) but was enthusiastic and very sympathetic to the Prince's work for education and art industry.

The financing of the scheme – optimistically estimated by Fuller at £30,000, Thomas Cubitt at £50,000, and more cautiously by enthusiasts at £75,000 – was a problem. Initially a loan was arranged from two contractors; but finally the money was raised by public subscriptions to guarantee a possible loss. The Queen gave £1,000 and Prince Albert £500, but the largest subscriptions came from industry, though painfully slowly.

The Prince spoke at a magnificent banquet given at the Mansion House on March 21, 1850. He put forward a vision of human progress:

> . . . we are living at a period of most wonderful transition, which tends rapidly to accomplish that great end, to which all history points – *the realisation of the unity of mankind.* Not a unity which breaks down the limits and levels the peculiar characteristics of the different nations of the earth, but rather a unity, the *result and product* of those very national and antagonistic qualities.
>
> The distances which separated the different nations . . . are rapidly vanishing before the achievements of modern invention, and we can traverse them with incredible ease; the languages of all nations are known . . .; thought is communicated with the rapidity, even by the power, of lightning. On the other hand, the *great principle of* division of labour, which may be called the moving power of civilisation, is being extended to all branches of science, industry and art . . .
>
> . . . the publicity of the present day causes that no sooner is a discovery or invention made than it is already improved upon and surpassed by competing efforts. The products of all quarters of the globe are placed at our disposal and we have only to choose which is the best and cheapest for our purposes, and the powers of production are intrusted to the stimulus of *competition and capital.*
>
> Gentlemen, the Exhibition of 1851 is to give us a true test and a living picture of the point of development at which the whole of mankind has arrived in this great task, and a new starting-point from which all nations will be able to direct their further exertions.[11]

This speech was well received but *Punch* could still portray him in June 1850 as *The Industrious Boy*, with a background of posters, trying to raise money, cap in hand.

There had already been trouble about the siting of the Exhibition: the previous year the Prince and Cole had agreed that the south side of Hyde Park would be the ideal venue, but this proposal raised a swarm of enemies. Colonel Sibthorp appointed

91 *The Industrious Boy:* 'Please to remember the Exposition'. The Prince was still appealing in June 1850 for financial support for the projected Exhibition.

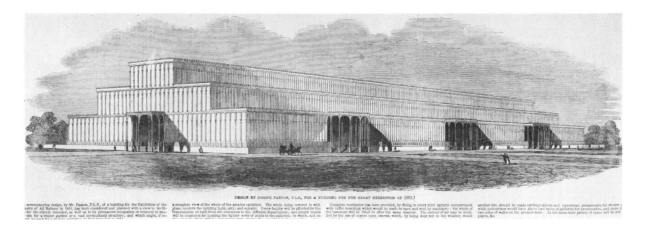

DESIGN BY JOSEPH PAXTON, F.L.S., FOR A BUILDING FOR THE GREAT EXHIBITION OF 1851.

92 Joseph Paxton's design for the Crystal Palace, first unveiled in the *Illustrated London News* on July 6, 1850.

93 Design for the proposed building in Hyde Park, from *Punch* July 1850.

himself the guardian of some threatened young elms; the inhabitants of Belgravia, Thomas Cubitt's smart new suburb, complained about losing even a small part of the park, while the fashionable inhabitants of Kensington and Tyburnia (modern Bayswater) were threatened with an invasion of undesirables who would ravish their silver and their serving maids.

This was the moment when Paxton came to the rescue, with his design based on the great Conservatory at Chatsworth, which promised both speed in erection and a much greater likelihood of removal. On July 15 the Committee accepted Paxton's universally admired scheme — he had published it in the *Illustrated London News* rather than submitting direct to the Committee. They had under ten months to the opening day on May 18, 1851. Granville had warned, in March, that a heavy load would fall on the

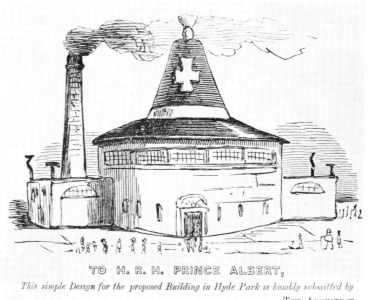

TO H. R. H. PRINCE ALBERT,

This simple Design for the proposed Building in Hyde Park is humbly submitted by

THE ARCHITECT.

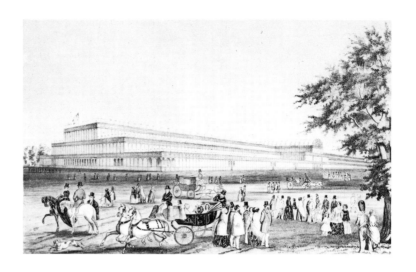

Prince, 'who appears to be the only person who has considered the subject both as a whole and in its details . . .'[12]

The goods for the Exhibition were selected by a number of committees, some working in countries or districts from which the goods came, others in London. They started arriving on February 12 – over 100,000 exhibits from a total of 13,937 exhibitors, of which 6,556 were foreign, the rest from the British Isles and the Empire.

Prince Albert complained to his grandmother of the strain: 'Just at present I am more dead than alive from overwork. The opponents of the Exhibition work with might and main to throw all the old women into panic and to drive myself crazy.'[13] There was a fear of plague because of the crowds; of civil disorder; of revolution on such a scale that indeed the King of Prussia forbade his brother and sister-in-law from coming to London because of the possible dangers. As the Prince wrote sardonically to him:

Mathematicians have calculated that the Crystal Palace will blow down in the first strong gale. Engineers that the Galleries would crash in and destroy the visitors; Political Economists have prophesied a scarcity of food in London owing to the vast concourse of people; Doctors that owing to so many races coming into contact with each other the Black Death of the Middle Ages would make its appearance as it did after the Crusades; Moralists that England would be affected by all the scourges of the civilised and uncivilised world; Theologians that this second Tower of Babel would draw upon it the vengeance of an offended God.

I can give no guarantee against these perils, nor am I in a position to assume responsibility for the possibly menaced lives of your Royal relatives . . .[14]

Despite these perils the Prince of Prussia came, as did many other foreign visitors.

However, the threat to the safety of the Queen had seemed so real that the initial scheme for the opening was to hold it in private. Again *The Times* led the protest: 'Where most Englishmen are gathered together there the Queen of England is most secure!' It was decided to allow in the public, but season-ticket holders only – with a healthy effect on sales. Over 25,000 ticket-holders thronged the building on the morning of May 1.

The Corps Diplomatique were unable to agree on the presentation of an address so it was therefore decided that they 'mute as fish, should pass before the Queen, make their bow, and stand on the platform, where they certainly did look like fish out of water'.[15] The note in the Prince's Journal for April 29 runs wearily: 'Terrible trouble with the arrangements for the opening.'

The royal party had a preview on April 30 and, as the Queen observed in her *Journal*, 'The noise and bustle was even greater than yesterday . . . and there is certainly still more to be done.' The Prince was still busy with last-minute preparations – 'my poor Albert is terribly fagged. All day some question or other or

94 Exterior view of the Crystal Palace in Hyde Park.

95 View of the transept and the glass fountain by Osler.

96 The Queen and Prince Albert's visit to
the Machinery Department of the Great
Exhibition. Working exhibits were a feature
of several departments.

Opposite
vi The Saltash Bridge, opened by the Prince
Consort in 1859. The Prince's standard can
be seen on the barge. The bridge was, of
course, designed by I. K. Brunel, but he was
too ill to attend the ceremony.

Colour picture, overleaf
vii *Salon de famille:* the Queen and the Prince
visited Louis Philippe and his family at the
Chateau d'Eu, in 1843. (Reproduced by
gracious permission of H.M. the Queen.)

some difficulty, all of which my beloved one takes with the
greatest quiet and good temper.'[16]

For the liveliest and most vivid description of the Opening one
has to turn again to the Queen herself;

The sight as we came to the centre where the steps and chair was placed,
facing the beautiful fountain was magic and impressive. The tremendous
cheering, the joy expressed in every face, the vastness of the building,
with all its decorations and exhibits, the sound of the organ (with 200
instruments and voices, which seemed nothing) and my beloved husband, the creator of this peace festival 'uniting the art and industry and
art of all nations of the earth', all this was moving, and a day to live for
ever. God gless my dear Albert, and my dear Country, which has shown
itself so great today.[17]

The success of the Great Exhibition of 1851 was bound to generate imitators, many of whom were sadly misled by its substantial
profit, something which no other nineteenth-century exhibition
achieved on the same scale, if at all. The Prince was never again
so intimately concerned with any other exposition, but he took a
great interest in the three projected in the next decade. The last
of these, that held in London in 1862, had been intended to be

part of a decennial series with the Great Exhibition, but this had
had to be postponed because of the unsettled state of international
affairs.

The Exhibition of Art-Industry in Dublin in 1853 was in fact
the end of a triennial series initiated by the Royal Dublin Society,
a parallel organization to the Royal Society of Arts, founded in
1731 for 'Improving Husbandry etc. . . .'. It was intended to
copy the Great Exhibition in a modest way: it, too, had a glass,
wood and iron building, similar in construction and design to the
Hyde Park building. It was much smaller but also had the large
double-height nave with aisles with galleries above. It stood on
one side of Merrion Square, presenting a front of some 300 feet.

It was designed by John Benson, an Irish architect who was
knighted after the opening, and promoted by William Dargan, a
successful railway contractor. Dargan, who even refused the
proffered knighthood, seems to have been a fairly disinterested
sponsor, guaranteeing the funds necessary for the building and
the organization, and undertaking to meet any loss at the end of
the exhibition. The industry represented was inevitably relatively
small, though a number of French firms, including Sèvres and
Aubusson, exhibited, and the West Midlands stalwarts from

97 Queen Victoria opening the Great
Exhibition on May 1, 1851. By H. C. Selous.

98 Visit of the Queen and the Prince to the Dublin Exhibition in August 1853. The Exhibition had been open all summer, and the Royal couple made a most successful visit to Dublin on their way to Scotland in the Royal yacht. From a watercolour by James Mahony.

99 The Great Tara Brooch, a facsimile made by Messrs Waterhouse of Dublin, an indication of the growing interest in the ancient arts of Ireland. Celtic jewellery was also exhibited in 1851.

England contributed – the Coalbrookdale company, Elkingtons, Copeland and Chance. Irish products were largely in the field of textiles – the famous tabinets of Dublin and the damasks of Belfast took pride of place, but there were also some examples of a new type of manufacture, Celtic jewellery made in imitation of the magnificent early masterpieces.

The Royal Dublin Society and the Secretaries, C. P. Roney and John C. Deane, did an impressive job, particularly in view of the relative poverty of the country and the appalling effects of the famine. Possibly the very lack of industry left more room for art. A large part of the building was occupied by an impressive collection of modern art, lent by a large number of owners. The Queen and the Prince sent their portraits by Winterhalter, and Mulready's *Wolf and Lamb*. A number of Irish landlords lent works, including the Duke of Devonshire, who sent Landseer's *Hawking* and *Bolton Abbey* and the Marquis of Lansdowne who sent Leslie's *Sir Roger de Coverley* and Stone's *Course of True Love*. English dealers and collectors also cooperated, indicating perhaps a degree of royal encouragement. Prince Albert's influence is also shown by the large group of Belgian works lent by King Leopold, and these supplemented by works from Holland, France and Germany provided, in the words of the *Art Journal*, an '*original* feature' and 'the most attractive portion of the Exhibition'.[18]

The Exhibition was opened on May 12 by the Irish Viceroy, the Earl of St. Germans. The royal family, who spent a week in Dublin at the end of August, visited the Exhibition every day, admiring the poplins, lace and pottery, and new methods of

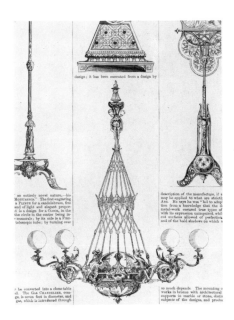

100 Gas chandelier designed by the architect, P. C. Hardwick, for the coffee room at the Great Western Hotel. Shown by the manufacturer Mr. Potts of Birmingham, one of the few English manufacturers to support the Dublin Exhibition.

hatching salmon, in which, the Queen noted in her *Journal*, 'Albert was especially interested as he is by every new and useful discovery.'[19] They called on Mr. Dargan to thank him for his help.

Four years later came the Manchester Art-Treasures Exhibition, even more overtly art-orientated. The Prince had been most anxious at the time of the 1851 Exhibition that works of art should be included, and had only been dissuaded from lack of room. When he was approached, therefore, by the promoters of this Exhibition, not only with a request to the Queen to lend some important works, but also to assist by encouraging other owners of important works to lend, too, he threw himself into the project with his usual enthusiasm.

'No country invests a larger amount of capital in works of art of all kinds than England;' he wrote to the Earl of Ellesmere, 'and in none almost is so little done for art-education. If the collection you propose to form were made to illustrate the history of art in a chronological and systematic arrangement, it would speak powerfully to the public mind, and enable in a practical way, the most uneducated eye to gather the lessons which ages of thought and scientific research have attempted to abstract . . .' He enclosed a catalogue which he had had prepared for the National Gallery Committee of 1853, and suggested that if the organizers took that as their outline for the Exhibition, it might be easier to persuade the owners of works of art of the seriousness of their purpose.[20] Whether it was the seriousness of the project or the royal example, the works were forthcoming, and a most impressive Exhibition was mounted.

It had sections dealing with ancient and modern paintings; one on historical miniatures; and one on British portraits; watercolours by living and dead masters; old master drawings. There was a sculpture gallery, and a special section displaying armour, most of which came from the famous Goodrich collection belong-

101 Manchester Exhibition — a general view of the nave showing the rows of paintings, from a Stereoscopic Co. view, now at the Manchester Art Gallery.

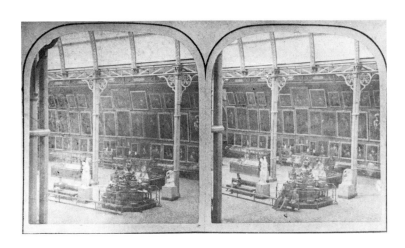

102 A very fine display of medieval armour was a feature of the Manchester Exhibition. Much of it came from the important collection of Samuel Meyrick of Goodrich Castle, Herefordshire.

ing to Samuel Meyrick, which included a suit of armour (seen in the centre of the picture above) now in the Wallace Collection. Decorative art played a smaller part than in 1851, but inevitably there was a Museum of Ornamental Art, collected and arranged by J. B. Waring, who later wrote the definitive work on the 1862 Exhibition. The Exhibition was brought up to date by a collection of photographs, several of which were lent by Prince Albert.

The Queen was unable to accompany the Prince to the opening, and so he has left a vivid picture of his visit, in a letter written after an exhausting day 'half dead with the day's fatigues'. He was staying with the Mayor at Abney Hall 'a house built upon a Gothic design and decorated by Mr. Crace, in the highest style of *luxe*, with the finest pictures, etc.' After a five-mile drive into Manchester, he opened the Exhibition, having received several addresses, each of which required an answer, and perambulated the building. He was then at liberty to inspect the actual exhibits, which he did for two hours, noting the presence of a number of familiar faces, including Carl Haag, one of the royal painters, Gustav Waagen, author of a guide-book to the Exhibition and an old friend of the Prince's, Playfair, Chadwick, Jacob Ominium, Lewis, and Eastlake. '. . . A wonderful collection,' he concluded, 'the building very beautiful and tastefully decorated the people very friendly . . .'[21]

The following day he was away at eight in the morning, to visit Salford, where he duly unveiled a statue of the Queen in Peel Park, after having received an address from the Corporation of Salford. By six o'clock that evening he was back at Buckingham Palace prepared to give his attention to the Queen's Speech for the opening of the new parliament.

The Manchester Exhibition of paintings and works of art pro-

103 The roodscreen designed for Hereford Cathedral by G. G. Scott, and manufactured by Skidmore's Art Manufactory Company, Coventry, exhibited in 1862. As engraved by J. B. Waring.

vided the first opportunity for artists and art historians to make comparisons. Many of these works were already available to the public, since so many country houses were open to respectable and serious students, but many were misattributed, and the chances for comparisons with other works by the same artist were rare. With the advent of photography of course, comparison of the actual paintings was no longer the only way to judge them but, even so, the Manchester Exhibition gave an opportunity for the display of works of art never before seen in public — and never again seen together. The usual spate of publications followed, giving the art-education element the widest possible exposure.

Prince Albert was less personally involved in the International Exhibition of 1862, which did in fact, of course, not open until after his death. Nonetheless, it was the logical successor to the 1851 Exhibition, seen by all at the time as the herald of a series of exhibitions which would gradually raise the standard of art and design, increase international cooperation and understanding, and generally enhance the march of human progress through scientific progress and art education.

Inevitably the later Exhibition has suffered from comparison with the earlier: Granville observed of Paxton, who had shown a desire to repeat his last-minute intervention of 1850, that he doubted that 'the same man can play the same game twice in his life with the same success', and perhaps this comment can be applied to the whole 1862 'team'. This did not include the Prince, Granville himself or Thomas Baring; Dilke survived from the 1851 Commission and, together with Thomas Fairbairn, Chairman of the Manchester Exhibition, and the Duke of Buckingham, was constituted a Trustee to manage the Exhibition. The prime mover was probably Henry Cole, who first organized support for the idea in the Society of Arts, and then involved his South Kensington team of designers, led by Francis Fowke, and supported by Townroe and Liddell.[22] The contractor was Kelk, who won the contract from four other firms in apparent open competition, but was generally known to be a friend and associate of Henry Cole.

The history of the 1862 Exhibition shows the lack of a single directing intelligence which could reconcile a number of desirable ends and control a number of strong personalities, each with their own objectives. Thus the Society of Arts was promoting a decennial exhibition, but Cole had the idea of using the project to provide a permanent building for his beloved South Kensington, incorporating both a great chorus-hall and picture galleries. The site chosen, that of the modern Natural History Museum, certainly affected the proposal for the large and elaborate gardens created by the Horticultural Society under Prince

104 Bust of the Prince Consort. The marble original was sculpted in 1849 by Baron Marochetti, and is now in the Royal Collection, Windsor Castle. A number of copies were made in metal, and more popularly in parian porcelain. One of these was exhibited in 1862.

Albert as President.

In March 1858, the Society of Arts agreed to work for an Exhibition to be held in 1861, but this had to be postponed because of the outbreak of hostilities between France and Austria. Cole arranged for Francis Fowke to prepare drawings and these were available to the Trustees in November 1860. Despite cries of jobbery, and Paxton's attempted intervention, the plans were accepted. They were based on Henry Cole's long-term requirements, including a hall rather larger than the Albert Hall, and proved so expensive that the construction had to be much modified, so that the hall was dropped, and a great deal of the fabric was temporary.

The Exhibition opened on May 1, 1862, in some confusion but was welcomed by exhibitors, and indeed by the public. In fact the total of $5\frac{1}{2}$ million visitors was only just below the 6 million of 1851; and any decrease was easily accounted for by the recent death of the Prince Consort, which meant no participation by the Queen, and no Royal visitors.

The exhibits were probably more varied and more interesting than those of 1851. They included photographic equipment and the electric telegraph, as well as manufacturing machinery of various sorts. The Art Journal recorded the most important objects, and J. B. Waring engraved the most prominent. Minton exhibited their monumental majolica fountain, some 36 feet high, designed by John Thomas, and a great technical achievement. Howell and James showed their ormolu objects, furniture manufacturers from all over Europe sent their wares, and of course porcelain, china and majolica all played an important part. An interesting element in this Exhibition were designs after objects which had been collected as a consequence of the Great Exhibition. Thus Minton showed majolica modelled after the Soulages Collection purchased by the South Kensington Museum, and exhibited at Manchester in 1857.

The designs of furniture manufacturers and upholsterers, textiles, carpets, metalwork, repoussé work, decorative leather, and ornamental slate, from all over Europe, America and even from Australia were supplemented with exotic sections. One of these was a Medieval Court, which had been a great attraction in 1851, and had been re-created at Sydenham. There was also a substantial section on oriental art, which later formed the nucleus of the South Kensington collections.[23]

The 1862 Exhibition was perhaps the logical outcome of the 1851. It seems less by comparison, but this was, perhaps, be-use of the absence of the controlling intelligence which had ade 1851 such a resounding success.

CHAPTER EIGHT

Albertopolis: The Creation of South Kensington

105 Cartoon for the roundel with the Prince's head,
in the Prince Consort Gallery, Victoria and Albert Museum.
Design by Godfrey Sykes.

The Great Exhibition was that rare thing, a great success. Over six million visitors came to see it, from all over England and even from abroad, by excursion train and organized parties. They came from all classes. They did not break the exhibits, behave in an unruly manner, or get drunk – possibly because alcoholic beverages were banned, or get plague – possibly because the water supplied was carefully filtered. The excellent arrangements made by the Executive Committee and the Commissioners had worked perfectly, while Colonel Sibthorp and *Punch* doubtless served to publicize the project.

The Exhibition closed on October 15, 1851, the anniversary of their engagement, the Queen noted, saddened because she did not go 'as a spectator' to see the closing. 'To think that all this great and bright time is past, like a dream, after all its success and triumph, and that all the labour and anxiety it caused for nearly 2 years should likewise now be only remembered as "a Has been" seems incredible and melancholy'.[1]

Meanwhile the Prince had not waited for the Exhibition to become a 'has been' before moving on to the next project. Before the Exhibition closed its doors and before the full extent of the surplus – some £180,000 – was known the Prince was discussing the employment of the money to found 'an Establishment in which by the application of Science and Art to industrial pursuits the Industry of all nations may be raised in the scale of human Employment, and where by the constant interchange of Ideas, Experience and its results each nation may gain and contribute something'.[2]

This project was the creation of 'South Kensington', that un-English complex of museums, scientific institutions, colleges of music and art, part university and part polytechnic, suffering from a crisis of identity from time to time, advancing in fits and starts. It is the Prince's greatest contribution of all to his adopted country. It is fair to say that it would have been more coherent and better-planned if its founder had survived for longer – the high hopes and comprehensive plans of the early years were succeeded by squabbling amongst the various institutions which had been united by the Prince's patronage.

The story of its development has been well told elsewhere, notably by the *Survey of London*, but it is important to note Prince Albert's early initiative. It was agreed after the 1851 Exhibition that the government would match the surplus and the Commissioners would remain in being to administer the estate to be purchased from the fund. By 1853, a complicated series of purchases and exchanges had put together the estate as we know it, and in August 1853 the Prince produced a plan and a memorandum. These were sent to a number of authorities for their comments.

106 The opening of the Royal Horticultural Gardens, June 5, 1861, by the Prince Consort, his last public function. It was a subdued occasion and the Queen was not present because of the recent death of the Duchess of Kent. This view shows the interior of the conservatory designed by Francis Fowke, with its terracotta ornament and polychromatic brickwork.

Comment was mixed and almost totally predictable: Granville was encouraging, Gladstone wrote to say no more money was available, Cole was worried about government control, while Barry was discouraging, suggesting that the National Gallery might not be prepared to move, though he thought South Kensington would do for scientific institutions.

Development began in two parts of the site, the centre was allocated for a central garden, ultimately developed by the Horticultural Society, of which the Prince became Prince-President. The dominant site, now occupied by the Albert Hall, was earmarked for the National Gallery, while that on the Cromwell Road, now the Natural History Museum, was first used for the International Exhibition Building of 1862.

The gardens were dominated by a conservatory and semicircular arcades on the northern side. When the 1862 building was erected, eastern and western galleries on either side of the garden were added, and these remained to provide further capacity for the South Kensington Museum.

The other part of the site on which development took place in Prince Albert's lifetime was the south-east corner, where a group of existing buildings stood between the newly built Brompton Church and the Old Brompton Road. These became the home of the South Kensington Museum a curious Albertian hybrid which is the ancestor of most of the institutions in South Kensington, and which exemplified the 'application of Science and Art to industrial pursuits' in a way which its founders intended and which the organizations which have followed have signally failed to do. It has since split into a large number of organizations which, more than anything else, bear tribute to the Prince Consort's ideas for English culture and education. This is not to say that some of these organizations might not have come into being without the Prince's intervention, but probably not in the same way or with such success.

The nucleus was the Government Schools of Design, founded in 1837 in an attempt to raise the low level of industrial design, and initially working in part of Somerset House. In 1852 Cole became Superintendent and, taking advantage of the Prince's support, he arranged to take over Marlborough House as home both for students and as museum of the practical arts. The collections included material from the 1851 Exhibition, as well as valuable objects designed to be exemplars for the students. The following year the remit of the schools was broadened to include science and they became the Department of Science and Art, directly responsible to the Privy Council Committee on Education. The Department was headed by a triumvirate of the Prince's men: Henry Cole, Lyon Playfair, from the Museum of Practical Geology, who became head of the Science Department,

Top, right

107 The Prince's original idea for a layout – the Commissioners later managed to complete their purchases at the north of the site. The scheme was strictly classical in layout, and the Prince explained that he himself inclined to 'an Italian or Palladian style of architecture'. Building A was the proposed National Gallery, estimated as some 190,000 square feet. B and C were suggested for Colleges of Art and Science. D and E were the Museums of Industrial Art, Patented Inventions, Trade Museums etc. K might be appropriated, he thought, to the Learned Societies 'as might express a wish to move'. I (the ground just being covered by the Ismaili Centre) could be given to the Academy of Music, for a Music Hall etc. (Memorandum by the Prince Consort, August 20, 1853, RA F.25/168.)

Bottom, right

108 The South Kensington Purchase showing the land bought with the surplus from the Exhibition of 1851. Most of it was undeveloped suburban land known as Brompton – it was Henry Cole's idea to christen it South Kensington.

Middle, top

109 The Sheepshanks Gallery at South Kensington, from an engraving of 1876. The gallery was designed in 1856 and contained the most up-to-date air conditioning arrangements to prevent damage to the pictures from gas illumination necessary to enable the gallery to open in the evenings for working men.

Far right, top

110 The Soulages Collection at Marlborough House, from a watercolour by William Casey at the Victoria and Albert Museum.

Middle, bottom

111 The Brompton Boilers, after a watercolour by J. C. Lanchenik 1863. The first buildings erected for the museum were temporary, of iron girders with corrugated iron roofs. They housed the exhibits from Marlborough House, an architectural museum, an educational collection, and a collection of patented industrial objects, thought to be of use to manufacturers.

Far right, bottom

112 The Educational Museum inside the Brompton Boilers, 1855. From a photograph in the collection of the Victoria and Albert Museum.

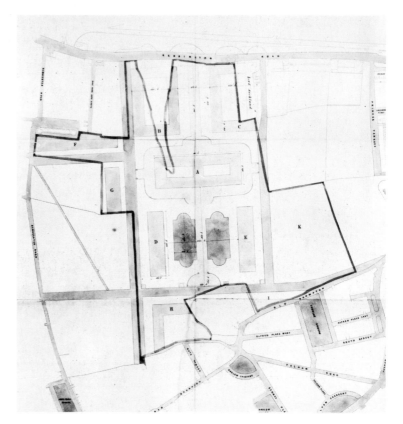

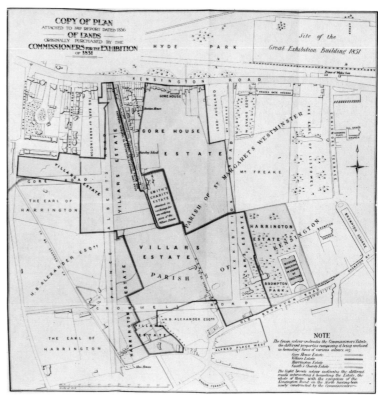

113 The funeral of the Duke of Wellington passing Apsley House, November 18, 1852. From a lithograph by T. Picken. The funeral car was designed by the School of Design students working under Cole and Redgrave, at the instigation of the Prince.

Opposite
114 The Royal family at Osborne, photographed by Caldesi for the Queen, about 1857. The Prince of Wales is on the right; on the Queen's lap is Beatrice, born in 1857; beside the Prince is Alfred, later Duke of Coburg, on the death of his uncle Ernest; behind the Queen is the Princess Royal, Victoria, who was to marry Prince Frederick William year. Also in the p 1843; Helena (18 Arthur (1850), late ... of Connaught; and, beside the Queen, Leopold (1853), later Duke of Albany.

and Richard Redgrave who was appointed Inspector of Art.

Under these three, the collections at South Kensington were built up, to include industrial and fine art, and also scientific material, both of pure scientific significance and also of industrial relevance, such as the material on fish culture and on the economic use of natural materials.

The art classes in London were supplemented by a system of provincial schools whose curricula and standards were established by Redgrave. The museum's collections were used as teaching material for them, and also made available by evening openings and lectures to working men. In due course the students became independent again in the form of the Royal College of Art, in 1897.

On the scientific side, the institution gradually attracted the teaching side of the College of Science and the Museum of Practical Geology, again running lectures for both full-time students and working men. The Prince was very interested in the need for lectures for working men, often attending these lectures himself.

The building expanded gradually under the stimulus of the interest in education, under a building team headed by the Engineer officer, Francis Fowke, who not only designed the Museum's new buildings but headed a practical team of Sappers who became the maintenance team, and helped to produce designs, and even provided the first photographers.

This rapid expansion slowed after the Prince's death in 1861, and even more after Cole's retirement in 1873. Both sides of the Department increased in size, till a split occurred at the end of the century. The Board of Education, created in 1899 took over the directly educational work, the scientific collections moved away; when the South Kensington Museum became the Victoria and Albert Museum, the new name was jealously restricted to the art side. The scientific teaching became the province of the new Imperial College founded in 1907.

In 1898, the Queen had suggested the new museum should be renamed the 'Albert Museum'. This would have been a proper tribute to the Prince, without whose initial support South Kensington would never have developed. It shows his capacity for identifying a need, and for choosing enthusiastic and hard-working allies to carry it out.

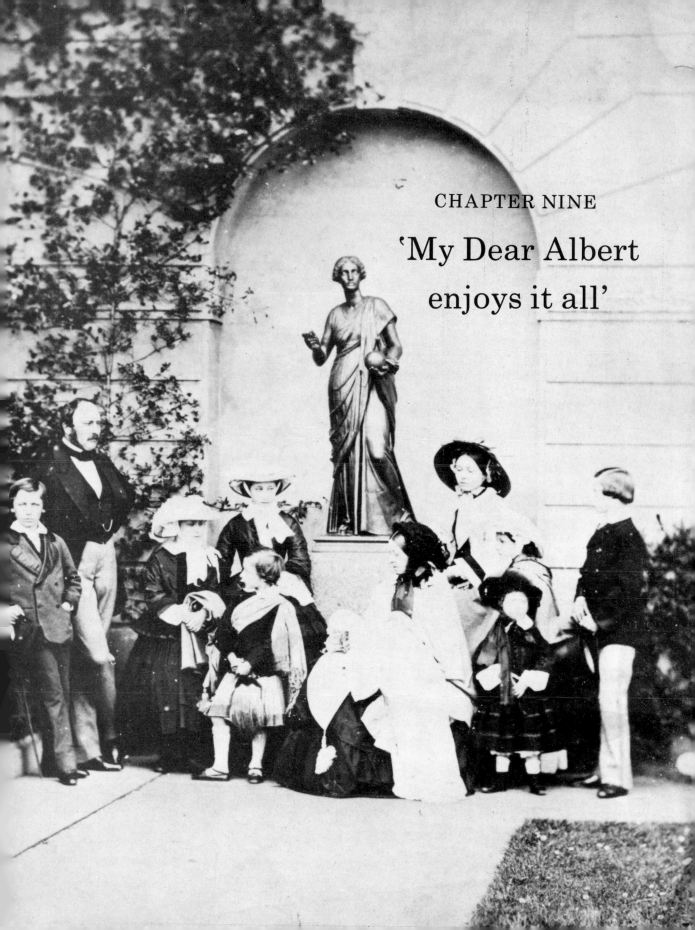

CHAPTER NINE

'My Dear Albert
enjoys it all'

'The Queen,' wrote Prince Albert tersely to the Chancellor of the Exchequer, 'is worse off than any sovereign of Europe, the small German princes included.'[1] He was referring to the state of Buckingham Palace, but he could have made that complaint about other aspects of the conditions under which the royal family lived.

Life at Court was a curious blend of the official and the domestic. In the early years of the Queen's reign the Prime Minister had been a regular visitor, dining frequently at Buckingham Palace, staying at Windsor, and accompanying the Queen on her amusements, forming part of the cavalcade of Ministers, ladies and gentlemen which followed the Queen into Windsor Great Park. Throughout her reign there was always a 'minister in attendance', often shivering on the heights above Balmoral or bored by Osborne, escorting her abroad to Germany or France; other Ministers and civil servants dined with the Queen and the Household when staying at Windsor. Foreign royalty were frequent visitors, either on state visits or privately.

In the same way the royal establishments were partially under the control of the Queen herself through the Privy Purse, which ran the financial side of the royal family's affairs, and partly under the control of the government, through the great officers of state. These dignitaries and, even more, their subordinates found cooperation beneath them, and this led to inconvenience, waste, indiscipline, and even danger to health. The reply to a complaint from the Queen herself that the dining-room was always cold, was '. . . properly speaking, it is not our fault, for the Lord Steward lays the fire only, and the Lord Chamberlain lights it . . .'[2] Another functionary described the plight of the Queen's guests, nine-tenths of whose suites could speak no English and who were left unattended by the Household staff: 'at Windsor Castle it constantly happens (when Her Majesty is retired for the evening) that visitors accost me in the Corridor, enquiring the way to their Apartments.'[3]

Three great officers of state, all political appointments, who had to be noblemen, adherents of one or other political party, were nominally in charge of different parts of the Household. The Lord Chamberlain controlled much of the palace, and was responsible for the housekeepers, housemaids and pages; much of the rest, excluding the grand halls, was under the control of the Lord Steward, including the cooks, porters and butlers, 'but whether the kitchen, sculleries, pantries, etc., remain under his charge . . . it is a question, which no one at this moment can reply to . . .'[4] The Master of the Horse was responsible for all the transport of the palace, the purchase, care, maintenance and training of an equine establishment amounting to several hundred animals, both ceremonial and day-to-day. He was, how-

115 *A Case of Real Distress. Punch*'s view of the Royal housing problem.

A CASE OF REAL DISTRESS.

ever, also in control of the footmen who worked in the palaces, as well as the coachmen, grooms and other male servants outside. External maintenance and building work, perpetually necessary in buildings several centuries old, was under the control of the Department of Woods, Works and Forests, Land Revenues etc., a particularly unsatisfactory part of the civil service at this period, which had been the subject of parliamentary investigation several times since 1800.

The situation became critical after the birth of the Princess Royal, and the Prince turned to Stockmar for advice. With his usual thoroughness, the Baron produced a report in January 1841, concluding that the 'principles on which the economy of the royal household are based, are inefficient, more calculated to produce anomalies and absurdities of all kinds, than the possibility of a sound, regular and effective administration.'[5]

With this evidence, the Prince asked Sir Robert Peel for help, embarrassing the Prime Minister who was anxious not to upset the aristocrats of either party who would expect to hold the Great Offices. He was too aware that attempts at reform in a traditionalist country were not popular, particularly from a minister who came from a middle-class manufacturing background, however affluent and cultured. The Prince responded with his usual good humour:

Much as I am inclined to treat the Household machine with a sort of reverence with its antiquity, I still remain convinced that it is clumsy in its original construction, and works so ill, that so long as its wheels are not mended there can neither be order nor regularity, comfort, security, nor outward dignity, in the Queen's Palace . . .[6]

116 The Queen's Audience Room at Windsor Castle, redecorated for her by the Prince.

Ultimately, the problem was amicably solved by improving the standing of the Master of the Household, an existing officer, but one whose authority was 'so undefined, limited, and partial, that the title is merely nominal . . . his office, as at present constituted, to all extents and purposes a nullity'.[7] He was given day-to-day control under the Great Officers, so that for the first time the domestic comfort of the sovereign was under the control of a single officer. This process took some time, for there were many vested interests. As Peel pointed out,

subordinate employees and their patrons of both political complexions are apt to make common cause against reform . . . by misrepresenting the motives of it, and provoking a clamour against it, in which the idle, the disappointed, the malicious, are quite ready to join. There are few enlisted on the other side . . . for practical well-considered reform in details excites . . . little active sympathy . . .[8]

The effect of the reorganization was also very beneficial financially. As Sir Robert Peel pointed out, in 1844, the Royal Household had entertained two unexpected royal state visits, without an additional grant, and the management of the royal finances was an example to her Ministers. This led to complaints that the Queen and the Prince were keeping patronage in their own hands, and possibly did not assist the Prince's later requests for a larger annuity. His parliamentary grant of £30,000 was extremely mean in view of the fact that Queen Adelaide had been granted £50,000 a year, but even when this ceased on her death in 1849, his allowance was not raised.[9]

Ultimately the solution was found in extensions which doubled the size of Buckingham Palace, and in the creation of two new privately owned homes for the royal family.

The Prince came from a family with a strong interest in architecture and decoration, and he had inherited his father's interest in building. He first turned his attention to Windsor, probably the favourite royal home in the early years of the Queen's married life.

Country life always had a great appeal for him as Lady Lyttelton observed:

... he is, if possible more ingenuous and sensible and gracious than ever; and he is as happy and cheerful now as he looked dull and sleepy in London. It is only that the poor man likes nothing but *das Landleben*, and she is so complying towards him that it may lead her to like it too at last ...[10]

Windsor Castle itself had been largely remodelled by Jeffrey Wyattville for George IV, and relatively little remained for the Prince to concern himself with as far as extensions and major alterations went. He was instrumental in saving a little fishing cottage at Virginia Water, and the remains of George IV's Royal Lodge, in which Anson was installed, from the civil servants who

117 *The Ballad of Windsor Chase. Punch*'s view of the Prince's Harriers. January 1844.

wanted them both cleared away. In August 1840, he wrote enthusiastically to his father: 'The new stables and the riding school will be magnificent. That long green space below the Terrace ... is to be laid out in pleasure grounds, with plants etc., and I shall occupy myself much with it.'[11]

Access to the Castle was improved some years later, and some homes clustering under the Castle walls were cleared, largely in the interests of hygiene. The 'pleasure grounds' between the Castle and the Park were improved, partly to give the royal family more privacy, though this led to some public protest over the stopping up of footpaths.

The drainage of the Castle gave cause for concern, and substantial sums were spent on both the drains and a better water supply in 1846.[12] Unfortunately this does not seem to have entirely solved the problem, for the Prince's death in 1861 is often blamed on the Castle drains.

In the early years of his married life he was more concerned with the Park than the interior of the Castle, but later some re-decoration was carried out under his control. He was responsible for the new look for the Queen's audience chamber, in 1857 employing a striking Jacobethan scheme. The Print Room was created for his use, and his diary records the way in which he started on the systematic cataloguing of the existing royal possessions.[13]

It was, however, in the Park itself that he left his greatest mark. He was appointed Ranger of Windsor Great Park in 1840, a role then relatively free of outside interference, and the post presented him with some of his greatest opportunities. The Park was only enclosed in 1817, and it had then been roughly divided into parkland still operated by the Crown, and farmland, some under royal control and some belonging to humbler agriculturists. The Prince threw himself into the creation of a working estate with all the thoroughness and enthusiasm of his nature.

The Park was extensive, stretching beyond Ascot racecourse to Sandhurst, and the Prince extended the royal holdings by purchasing land and sporting rights in the vicinity. The Park provided much needed recreation in the form of sport, as well as an opportunity to farm. There were the Royal buckhounds, hunting the Park deer of which a few hundreds remained. The Prince had a pack of beagles or harriers whose meets were attended by the Queen and her ladies as well as by guests and Ministers. He was also fond of 'flying off coursing on foot' with his grey-hounds,[14] particularly the beloved Eos. There were shooting parties after pheasant for which the Prince kept a pack of Clumber spaniels. Both official and unofficial visitors would be taken out, and there are many mentions in his diary of 'a grande chasse'.

The Prince's sporting activities did not go uncriticized. *Punch*,

118 Eos, a favourite greyhound, painted by Landseer.

which accepted fox-hunting, taking Mr. Jorrocks' view that it was the 'image of war without its guilt, and only twenty-five per cent of the danger', could not stomach the idea of stag-shooting particularly as practised in Germany. The Queen was savagely pilloried for her attendance at a traditional German *battue* organized by her hosts on their visit to Coburg in 1845. It was compared to Queen Elizabeth's liking for bear-baiting.[15]

The *Ballad of Windsor Chase*, published in 1844, portrayed the Court out hunting with plump beagles and stouter huntsmen, pursuing bagged hares, followed by the Queen in her phaeton, Anson, and the other gentlemen on horseback, and three maids-of-honour in another carriage.

Improvements to the pleasure grounds were put in hand in 1840, and these included a new aviary, and new kennels for the royal pet dogs. The Queen had lavished her affection on the spaniel, Dash, during her lonely adolescence, recording her attention to his bath, even on the day of her coronation. He was succeeded by a number of other dogs, including the stupid terrier Islay, so despised by Lord Melbourne, and Noble and others who brightened her widowhood. The Prince brought his greyhound, Eos, with him, and she was succeeded by others. There were also a number of German 'dachs' dogs, and a selection of other terriers.[16]

Within the Park, the Prince's farming was characteristically well-organized and unfashionably hard-headed. His farming, like the rest of his activities, was intended to show results and to be an example to others. He took on two farms on his marriage, the Norfolk and Flemish farms, but did not obtain the reversion

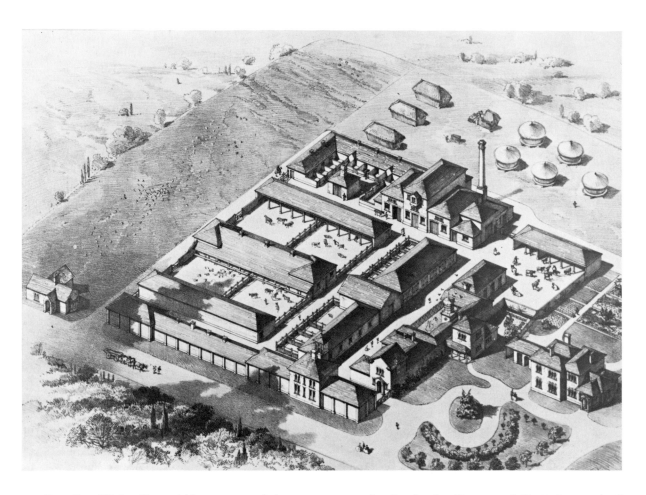

119 *Home Farm Windsor.* The model home-
stead designed by A. G. Dean for the Prince
Consort. From A. G. Dean's *Selected Designs
for Country Residences* etc. (1867). Note the
covered buildings for stock, the steam engine
which carried out mechanical tasks like
chaff-cutting and root-slicing, and the
pigeoncote on the bottom right of the
picture.

of the two nearest the Castle, the Home and Shaw farms, until
1849. From this date he gradually improved the buildings on all
the farmsteads, employing an acknowledged expert A. G. Dean
to design some of the buildings.[17] The most elaborate buildings
were erected at the Home farm, including accommodation for his
prized herd of white 'Windsor' pigs, the most successful of his
prizewinning farm stock, of which he was exhibiting as early as
1843. He also had a herd of Berkshire pigs. These buildings in-
corporated all the most up-to-date ideas, and the Prince himself
experimented with different types of pens for fattening cattle.

For the interior of the dairy building he turned to John Thomas,
a sculptor and architect already working on the gateways to
Buckingham Palace. The interior is a riot of Minton tiles, with
medallions incorporating portraits of the royal family and animal
motifs. Again hygiene goes hand in hand with art: the Wedg-
wood cream pans sit on marble shelves, while the atmosphere is
cooled by the water flowing from John Thomas's fountain. The
stained glass windows exclude light while the coffered ceiling of
pierced tiles provides ventilation.

The other farms are less elaborate, partly because the buildings were intended to be an example to Royal tenants, and therefore were not designed to be expensive. He added a large workshop complex in the Park. Each farm had a different type of stock: thus he had three herds of fattening cattle, Herefords at Shaw farm, Devon cattle at Norfolk farm, and Shorthorns at the Flemish farm.

He joined the Smithfield Club, one of the oldest and most aristocratic of agricultural organizations, presided over since its foundation in 1798 by a series of great Whig landowners. Its objectives were the improvement of cattle and sheep fattened on both grass, hay and roots, and on corn and cake, and it held annual shows in December, for fat stock of all kinds.[18] Prince Albert first visited the Show in 1840, often taking the Queen and the children in later years, but he did not start exhibiting till 1843. Inevitably the first animals he exhibited were bought in,

120 Sketch for the interior of the Royal Dairy, by John Thomas. The designs were carried out largely in Minton tiles.

121 Smithfield Show 1850: *Bringing in implements*. The Prince was insistent on the importance of mechanized agriculture, and used the most up-to-date methods on his own farms.

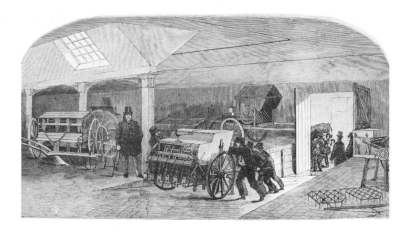

122 Ploughing: the Smith System. The early steam engines were too heavy to transport across arable land, so the plough was dragged across the ground through a system of cables. The Prince originally employed a Smith plough at Windsor, and then later moved it to Osborne.

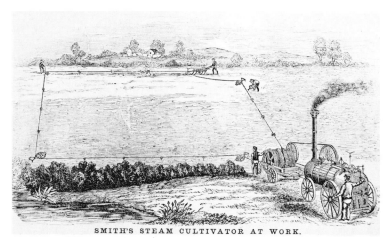

SMITH'S STEAM CULTIVATOR AT WORK.

123 *Bringing in a fat pig*. The Prince won a number of prizes throughout the country for his Windsor pigs.

and then fattened on the Windsor farms, though by 1859, he was exhibiting Devons, Herefords and Shorthorn cattle, all of his own breeding.

He also exhibited widely elsewhere, encouraging the foundation of other fatstock shows, such as that at Birmingham, founded in 1849 to which he sent Major Wemyss, his manager at Windsor, with a £50 donation. He showed his usual interest in Ireland, becoming a subscriber to the Royal Agricultural Improvement Society in Dublin in 1844, and received a Silver Medal for a long-horned cow exhibited that year, continuing to exhibit there in the following years. He was presented with a gold medal for his 'attention to the interests of the Society'.

In 1855, he sent a number of animals to the Paris Show, winning first prize for a home-bred Devon heifer, Bessy; also other prizes for cattle, a second prize for a pen of his Windsor pigs, and for a pen of Brahma-Pootra hens. With characteristic enthusiasm, he left the prizes in France to be competed for in the following year. Two years later he entertained the Emperor of the French at Osborne House. Inspired by his royal host's example, the diplomatic Emperor decided to form a herd of Shorthorn cattle, and a flock of Southdown sheep, and they were purchased for him by the Prince's farm managers at Osborne and Windsor.

Prince Albert also joined the recently founded Royal Agricultural Society of England, becoming a life governor. He attended a number of their meetings, being guest speaker at the dinner in 1851, and was indeed President at the time of his death. He presided over two meetings during 1861, and characteristically opened the meetings to reporters during his term of office, so that there should be a wider ventilation of the agricultural subjects under discussion.[19]

He saw, perhaps more clearly than the great Whig proprietors, that farming had to become more scientific to compete with foreign produce. As he reminded the members of the Society meeting at York in 1848,

Science and mechanical improvements have in these days changed the mere practice of cultivating the soil into an industrial pursuit, requiring capital, machinery, industry and skill, and perseverance in the struggle of competition . . . we must consider it a great progress, as it demands higher efforts and a higher intelligence . . .[20]

The Royal Show, then an exhibition which moved round the country, was held in Windsor Great Park in 1851. In 1862, the Show was to be held in Battersea Park, and he hoped that, in keeping with the 1862 Exhibition, it would have an international flavour, warning the Council against 'island prejudices' and reminding them that international attendance would swell the gate.

124 The Royal Hereford ox, painted by F. W. Keyl, a pupil of Landseer, for the Royal family.

125 Prince Albert's Windsor pigs. From a watercolour by F. W. Keyl.

The role of landlord gave the Prince an opportunity to put his philanthropic principles into practice. He was particularly concerned that his own labourers' conditions should be as good as possible, both from the quality of their housing, and the nearness of their housing to their place of work. He built a number of cottages at Windsor for his workmen, and was also most interested in educational facilities for them, both for the men themselves and for their children. A school, maintained at the Queen's expense, was provided for both boys and girls, and the Prince concerned himself personally with adult education for his workmen.[21]

He founded the Windsor Association, which gave prizes for

the best kept cottages to encourage the men and their wives to make the best of their new accommodation. An annual fête was held at the Great Park, until after the Queen's death.

The royal family had the use of two other residences away from Windsor. One was 'dear Claremont', the English home of King Leopold, which had fond childhood memories for the Queen. This was lent to them in the early years of marriage and gave them a much needed break from official life and its vexations at Windsor. The other was the Prince Regent's 'marine residence', the Brighton Pavilion, which proved increasingly unsuitable for a young married Queen with small children. Its position in the centre of rapidly expanding Brighton made privacy impossible: the *Illustrated London News* reported that the Queen could not 'enjoy a walk without being subjected to annoyances . . .' It was not surprising that, by November 1843, the idea of a new more secluded marine residence was being discussed by the Prince and Peel. The choice fell on Osborne House in the Isle of Wight, not far from Norris Castle, a childhood haunt of the Queen, which she and the Prince had visited in the previous August.

The Prince saw Osborne for the first time in March 1844, and it was taken on lease for a year. The Queen herself did not see it until August, after the birth of Prince Alfred, her fourth child. She was enthusiastic about the project, and negotiations for the purchase began that autumn. Uncle Leopold was kept informed, and in March 1845, the Queen could write:

126 Thomas Cubitt, the London developer and contractor, whom Prince Albert chose to design and build Osborne House, and to build the massive eastern and southern extensions to Buckingham Palace. 'Osborne must ever be bound up for us with the memory of this excellent, excellent man, who executed and aided in carrying out all my beloved Albert's plans.'

. . . we have succeeded in purchasing Osborne in the Isle of Wight, and . . . we shall probably run down there before we return to Town, for three nights. It sounds so snug and nice to have a place of one's own, quiet and retired, and free from all Woods and Forests, and other charming departments who really are the plague of one's life.[22]

Osborne House appealed to the Prince for a number of reasons, which he set out in a memorandum to Peel. Its situation seemed ideal because of its healthiness, the good water supply and drainage, its nearness to the navy at Portsmouth, and its convenience for marine excursions, for which the Queen had just acquired a new steam yacht. He also looked forward to improving the estate farms which were neglected, and to making new plantations — clearly this private estate would offer him new opportunities as a model landlord, and the complete freedom denied to him at Windsor under the eye of the Department of Woods and Forests.[23]

The original intention was merely to repair and possibly extend the house, a relatively modest mansion of some 16 bedrooms, and for this Prince Albert flouted convention and turned, not to an architect, but to a well-known London builder. Thomas Cubitt (1788–1855) had made his name as a developer, par-

127 Design for the New House at Osborne, 1845, by Thomas Cubitt. A drawing done for the Queen and Prince, and now in the Royal Library at Windsor. This shows the house substantially as built, but the balcony above the Marble Corridor on the right-hand block had a first storey open-range added, providing further communication between the Pavilion block on the left and the Household block on the right.

ticularly in the building of Belgravia, the smart suburb close to Buckingham Palace, and he had also given evidence to a number of parliamentary commissions on questions connected with town planning, the construction industry and problems of urban hygiene. He had come into contact with the royal family when the Queen had taken a house in Belgrave Square for her mother in 1840, and a number of the Prince's gentlemen lived in Belgravia in houses built by him.[24]

The Prince sent for Cubitt at Christmas 1844, and asked for a report on the house. Cubitt's survey was thorough but discouraging, or perhaps he merely interpreted his royal clients' instructions correctly. He reported that the house 'could not be converted by mere alterations and repairs into a Residence affording even that modest degree of accommodation . . . but that the construction of a new House is indispensably necessary and would be less expensive in the end than the repair of the present.'[28]

The decision was taken to build afresh but meanwhile Cubitt was instructed to repaper and paint the old house for the royal family's immediate occupation. The Prince selected the wallpapers himself, and also inspected Cubitt's works, and two of his most recently completed houses in Belgravia. Sir Robert Peel accompanied the royal couple to Osborne after Easter, and the Prince walked him all round the property, doubtless discussing his proposed improvements. Thomas Cubitt also waited on the Prince, and on this occasion the Prince made 'with him a building plan'. Cubitt submitted a design for the new house in April 1845, but this was clearly later altered by the Prince in detail, the storeys being made slightly higher, and the new-classical details more academically correct.

Some embarrassment has been caused to architectural commentators, both at the time and in our day, by the decision to employ Cubitt under direct control, probably with the advice of Gruner, rather than a well-known architect.[26] It is the more interesting since the Prince was already in touch with the newly formed Royal Institute of British Architects, where he had presented prizes in April 1843, and he must have met all the leading architects, either through the Fine Art Commission and the Palace of Westminster or through the work being done at Windsor or Buckingham Palace. With the benefit of hindsight and in view of the subsequent trouble with Edward Blore over the east wing of Buckingham Palace, one can only feel that the Prince's judgement was sound.

The relationship with Thomas Cubitt was a very happy one, which lasted until his death in 1856. The Prince came to rely on his judgement, and consulted him on a number of subjects not directly connected with building works, such as the South Kensington purchase. Cubitt became more a friend than a builder, he was invited up to the Osborne nursery at the Queen's command to see the 'infant princess'. When, in due course, he bought himself a country estate in Surrey the Prince took time off, in the

128 The Billiard Room, Osborne. From a photograph of 1867. The marble statues include those of the Royal children in allegorical costume, by Mary Thornycroft; the billiard table itself was made by Thurston, to the Prince's own design, and is of slate marble according to Eugene Magnus's patent system. In front of the pillar on the right can be seen the table by Elkington, made for Prince Albert and exhibited at the Great Exhibition.

129 The Prince's Dressing Room and Bath Room at Osborne. From a photograph of 1875. The picture is *Hercules and Omphale* by Gegenbaur, bought in 1844.

busy summer of 1851, to plant some rare conifers in the grounds at Denbies. Cubitt was even supplied with pigs from Windsor.

The new house at Osborne was commodious and cleverly designed to provide a private pavilion for the Queen's immediate family, extensive suites of guest rooms in the 'Main Wing', and a Household wing for the numerous ladies and gentlemen in waiting. Even so, a number of cottages were added to the estate, to provide accommodation for the Queen's numerous relations. Its Italianate style is reputed to have been chosen by the Prince because the view from the Osborne slopes reminded him of the Bay of Naples, though it also echoes Cubitt's London houses. Internally the decoration clearly owes much to both Gruner and the Prince. The planning of the house is very up-to-date with its lofty well-ventilated rooms looking on to the broad terraces; ample discreet service accommodation is hidden away in a light basement. The main reception rooms are hardly palatial, and the private apartments on the first floor are modest. However, they were well equipped and bathrooms for the Queen and the Prince were installed. On the top floor there were airy nurseries for the younger children.

The house was filled with works of art purchased by the Prince: a portrait of the family by Winterhalter, statues of the children by Mary Thornycroft, and his own statue in Roman armour by Emil Wolff. William Dyce was commissioned to paint a fresco of *Neptune entrusting the Command of the Sea to Britannia* for the grand staircase. There were objects which had been shown at the Great Exhibition, a pair of glass candelabra by

Osler, an electroplate stand by Elkington. A billiard table for Osborne was designed by the Prince Consort himself, and made by Thurston, out of slate enamelled to resemble marble by the process patented by Eugene Magnus. Most important and interesting of all were the Prince's own purchases of early Italian paintings as well as works by later masters such as Mantegna, Giorgione and Bellini.

Though Prince Albert installed an organ at Buckingham Palace, and also enjoyed playing the one at Windsor, he had to be content with a piano and a humble harmonium at Osborne.

In the grounds at Osborne, the Prince showed the same interest for improvement, supervising the setting-out of the ter-

130 The Swiss Cottage and Museum at Osborne. The cottage was imported from Germany and erected in England, in memory of the Switzerei at the Schloss Rosenau. The children were given the cottage as a playhouse, complete with kitchen, upstairs dining room and even a miniature shop. The museum became the repository for objects brought back by the children from visits, and for some of the lesser gifts made to the Royal family.

races, planting trees and shrubs, seeing the expert on water and drainage himself, making plans for sewage disposal, looking over his farming operations. The Queen enjoyed seeing him so happy: 'It does my heart good to see how my beloved Albert enjoys it all, and is so full of admiration of the place, and of all the plans and improvements he means to carry out. He is hardly to be kept at home for a moment.'[27]

There were also buildings to be restored on the estate, the large Elizabethan Barton farm, bought for its land, and almost as an annexe for extra guests, and Whippingham Church.

The improvement of Buckingham Palace presented a more intractable problem. Osborne House was privately owned and could be paid for out of the economies effected by the Prince's household reforms: any major improvements to Buckingham Palace would have to be paid for by parliamentary vote. Not only was it a time of great national depressions, but payments for the London residence of the sovereign had been an irritation to the House of Commons for nearly a quarter of a century.

George IV had started works on Buckingham House, soon after his accession in 1820, and through extravagance and mismanagement he and his chosen architect, John Nash, had spent over half a million pounds during his reign.[28] It was not completed or even habitable on his death, and a further £150,000 had to be spent. Edward Blore, an architect best known for his Gothic country house practice, whose chief recommendation at this stage was the fact that he was in no way connected with Nash or any of George IV's building activities, was commissioned to make it ready for William IV. The latter had always disliked his brother's palace, and in fact died before it was ready, so it was the young Queen Victoria who moved in on July 13, 1837.[29]

A number of piecemeal alterations were carried out to make the Palace more suitable for a young Queen with a growing family. The hygenic conditions gave cause for concern, partly because of the presence of a major sewer under the forecourt. Dr. Lyon Playfair was called in, and found the curious smells which had caused so much concern amply explained by the lack of ventilation and untrapped sewer gullies. The condition of the royal kitchens he found rather worse than some places found by the Commission reporting on the state of large towns under Edwin Chadwick, of which he was a member.[30] Improvements were made in the drains and to the offices, but for the first decade of her reign the Queen had to manage in the inconvenient Palace she had inherited, something which must have increased the dislike of London felt by her husband.

Prince Albert made a number of artistic and other improvements, and one of the first things he put in hand was the creation of a new chapel in the southern conservatory on the Garden Front (now the Queen's Gallery). It was consecrated in March 1843, by the Archbishop of Canterbury, and shortly after the Prince made arrangements for a domestic chaplain, appointing the Honorable and Reverend C. L. Courtenay, in the following month.[31]

The Grand Staircase was redecorated in a grand neo-classical manner, in 1845, under the supervision of Ludwig Gruner, the Prince's adviser on art.[32] These improvements doubtless made the Palace more agreeable but did not solve the basic problem which was one of space. The Queen complained again to Peel in February 1845. As she knew, he was 'already acquainted with the state of the Palace and the total want of accommodation for our little family which is growing up' and the time that any new building would take to complete. She went on:

... most parts of the Palace are in a sad state, and will ere long require a further outlay to render them *decent* for the occupation of the Royal Family or any visitors ... A room containing a larger number of those persons whom the Queen has to invite ... to balls, concerts, etc. .... is much wanted. Equally so, improved offices and servants' room, the want of which put the departments of the household to great expense yearly ...[33]

131 Buckingham Palace in 1846, after the alterations made by John Nash for George IV, with the Marble Arch in its original position. Watercolour painted for the Queen by Joseph Nash, and now in the Royal Collection.

132 Buckingham Palace in 1852. From a lithograph by E. Walker, showing Blore's new front which closed off Nash's courtyard. The Marble Arch was moved to its present position.

Peel merely replied that, in view of the imminent imposition of the Income Tax, this was not a judicious moment to introduce any expensive scheme for the Palace, a view borne out by *Punch*'s comment. It was not until the following May that six Commissioners for the Enlargement of Buckingham Palace were appointed, each representing some department or interest that would have to approve any works. The Prime Minister, the Chancellor of the Exchequer, and the Chief Commissioner of Woods and Forests, from the department of states responsible for palaces, were all appointed *ex officio*. Artistic opinion was to be given voice by Earl de Grey, a noted amateur architect and first President of the newly formed Royal Institute of British Architects; by Francis Egerton, later Lord Ellesmere, owner of the great Bridgewater Collection of paintings; and by Lord Lincoln, later fifth Duke of Newcastle, a great landlord in the Dukeries, and a former Commissioner. Blore was again appointed architect, and the House of Commons voted £150,000 for the enlargement of the Palace.

Victory for the Prince was the appointment of Thomas Cubitt, as contractor for the building. He had just seen the Queen and the Prince into the newly completed Pavilion at Osborne in September 1846, and had clearly impressed the Prince by his ability to keep to both price and time schedules. Blore may well have felt that to deal with one known large contractor of standing would be easier than the traditional mixture of specialist tradesmen, each carrying out one type of building work with all the friction and uncertainty that that meant.

The design for the additions to the Palace was carried out by Blore, though the Prince had many discussions with the sympathetic Peel, sketching out his designs. Essentially, the scheme was to close in the east side of Nash's great open courtyard, a practical and convenient solution which improved the communications in the Palace, but which deprived Londoners of one of their few dramatic architectural compositions. The *Builder* was no admirer of the existing Palace: '. . . [it] is *not* a worthy residence for the sovereign of this country: ever since its erection it has been a complete disgrace to the nation from an architectural point of view; . . . whether it be taken externally with its most unpicturesque outline, or internally, with . . . the puerility of its details . . .'[34] The new plans were unveiled in 1847, and the editor was no better pleased, observing that 'the design does not pretend to grandeur or magnificence, scarcely to dignity;' adding that 'the architect was probably right in attempting . . . little more than an ordinary piece of street architecture in stone instead of stucco . . .'[35] However, others may feel with the *Builder*'s readers that grandeur and magnificence are things to be looked for in the sovereign's palace, and Blore's façade is certainly dis-

133 The Pavilion Breakfast Room at Buckingham Palace. After a watercolour by J. Roberts, 1850. The furniture and decoration came from Brighton Pavilion when it was dismantled in 1847. They were installed at Buckingham Palace at the insistence of the Prince, who refused any suggestion from the architect, Edward Blore, that he should design modern mantelpieces and fittings.

Left

xiv State Ball at Buckingham Palace, July 5, 1848, showing the new decorations to the Grand Staircase, decorated under the supervision of Ludwig Gruner. From a watercolour by Eugene Lami. (Reproduced by gracious permission of H.M. the Queen.)

appointing. It was said to have been derived from Caserta, the country palace of the Bourbon rulers of southern Italy, which the Prince may have seen on his brief visit to Italy in 1839. There is no evidence, however, that he suggested this to Blore, though presumably he had to approve the designs, together with the Commissioners, and he must bear some responsibility for the unhappy result. Blore's façade did not survive very long, for like other contemporary architects, he was lured by the blandishments of French quarry owners to use Caen stone, which though cheap and easily worked was rapidly destroyed by the London atmosphere. Even before the building was completed the sentries were menaced by falling pieces of stone, and the solution was to paint the stone façade as if it had been Nash's despised stucco. In 1912, a new façade in Portland stone designed by Aston Webb in accordance with the Georgian tastes of the day, replaced that designed by Blore.[36]

As the new wing to Buckingham Palace was rising, so the interior of the Brighton Pavilion was being dismantled, since the alterations to Buckingham Palace were to be financed partly through the sale of the site of the Pavilion for building development. The Prince planned to make use of the magnificent fittings for the new reception rooms. The small dining-room, created for the royal family's private use, contained the exotic mantel-piece from Brighton, as well as other salvaged items. Here the Prince took a great interest, personally approving the magnificent grate. Together with the mantelpiece came the Chinese furniture, much of which had been designed originally for the Prince Regent's earlier palace at Carlton House. This is another interesting example of the Prince's liking for Carlton House furniture, which he had in his sitting room at Windsor. Posterity is very much indebted to the Prince Consort for the rescue of one of the finest collections of Chinoiserie in England, for though the Brighton Town Commissioners ultimately roused themselves to save the Pavilion, there is no evidence that they would have been able or willing to preserve all the rooms complete with their costly fittings.[37]

Inevitably there was confusion about the financial responsibility for the new building, and the divisions between the departments of the Household again reared their heads. Despite these vicissitudes the Palace was completed, with rooms for the servants above and below: cubicled attics on the top floor for the maidservants, and valets' rooms for visiting servants in the mezzanine. On the *piano nobile* there were more reception rooms furnished from Brighton, including the famous central Balcony room, and more grand bedrooms for important visitors; above there were nurseries and more visitors' rooms. Prince Albert could write to his brother Duke Ernest who was coming to London for the Princess Royal's wedding in 1858: '. . . It will be a triumph to find room for all the guests . . . in Buckingham Palace!!' Even so he had to add, 'We cannot put up any gentlemen, and we beg you to bring as few servants as possible. You will have to be satisfied with very little room . . .'[38]

A new suite of entertaining rooms was also required, and this was built on the south side of the Palace between 1851 and 1856. Here the Prince's own control was considerable, though his attempt to avoid official interference by appointing Cubitt without any architect was defeated. Lord John Manners the newly appointed Minister of Works seems to have been responsible for the appointment of James Pennethorne as architect for the design of the exterior of the building, though the interior seems to have been entrusted to Ludwig Gruner, as usual. The south wing contained a ballroom and ball supper room, connected by a series of grand galleries. Much needed new kitchen accommodation was also provided.

Royal entertaining was at this time an important part of the social scene, and was also intimately connected with political and official life. Convenient rooms for entertaining on a large scale had been needed for a long time, as had been accommodation for important official visitors like the Emperor Louis

134 Lithograph of the Supper Room at Buckingham Palace, from Pennethorne's drawings for the south wing. The decoration for the new wing was most carefully chosen, and Pennethorne's design for the plaster ceilings and walls were engraved, then coloured in various ways by young men working in Gruner's studio, and submitted for approval.

Napoleon and the Empress Eugenie, for whose visit in 1854 the new rooms in the front of Buckingham Palace were used.

The new ballroom reflected the Prince's interest in Raphael and in Italianate decoration generally. Ludwig Gruner and Pennethorne prepared a series of engravings of the proposed decorations, and various colour schemes were tried out. The final scheme was based on the Cinquecento style, and was of incredible richness and elaboration. The lower part of the walls were hung with silk decorated with the national devices in flowers while above there were panels filled with rather over-life-size copies of the *Hours*, after Raphael, copied in Rome by Professor Canzoni.

The Queen's 'fine new room' was opened with a ball on May 8, 1856, and both she and the Prince were delighted with it. The room was convenient, the red benches along either wall provided ample accommodation and the elaborate ventilation arrangements worked. In the Queen's own words: 'everyone could rest and everyone could see. It was truly a most successful Fête, and everyone was in great admiration of the rooms.'[39]

The suite was completed by an equally elaborate supper room decorated to resemble the interior of a tent.

A large blue velarium, sown with golden stars, and bordered by cords and arabesques, extends over the whole of the dome, and it is painted as if the sky were seen beyond, between the cords which tie it down at the foot ... The walls of the upper part of the room are divided into panels alternately painted with arabesques in colour, on a red ground, and with

135 Prince Albert in Highland dress. Engraved by Barlow after a portrait by John Phillip.

the royal arms in chiaroscuro on a gold ground. The north and south sides contain a frieze in relief . . .'[40]

This was based on Raphael's *History of Psyche*, with additions by Gibson, the whole being executed by Theed, and enriched with painting to simulate marble.

Both rooms were ruthlessly re-decorated for Edward VII by Bessant, the richly decorated walls being swept away and re-placed by a scheme of red, white and gold. The organ survives in the ballroom, but it is not now in use.

The acquisition of a home in the Highlands was not as deliberate as the purchase of Osborne. The Queen and the Prince made several Scottish excursions before they found Deeside, though *Punch*, as always on the lookout for ways of lampooning Albert, detected his interest in Scotland very early on. 'Just kilted at Blair Athol,' was a comment on the second royal trip to the Highlands, in the autumn of 1844, when the royal couple took Blair Castle from Lord Glenlyon.

The Queen had first seen Scotland in 1842, when she had travelled north in the antiquated *Royal George*, the last royal yacht dependent on sail. She had been laid low by the rough weather and when she arrived off Leith, the Mayor of Edinburgh was not there to greet her. Even so, she was enchanted by her first sight of Edinburgh: '. . . it is quite beautiful, totally unlike anything else I have seen; and what is even more, Albert, who has seen so much, says it is unlike anything *he* ever saw; it is so regular, everything built of massive stone, there is not a brick to be seen.'[41]

Holyroodhouse, the royal Palace in the heart of Edinburgh, was as yet unrestored, and the royal couple stayed in the Duke of Buccleugh's Dalkeith Palace, just outside Edinburgh. The Queen wrote enthusiastically in her diary of the 'different charac-ter' of the country and the people, and recorded Albert's reaction which was to find in both a resemblance to Germany. They moved on to Taymouth Castle where Prince Albert went stalk-ing with Lord Breadalbane, a pursuit which he found 'one of the most fatiguing, but it is also one of the most interesting . . . There is not a tree, or a bush, behind which you can hide yourself . . . One has, therefore, to be constantly on the alert in order to cir-cumvent them; and to keep under the hill out of their wind, crawling on hands and knees, dressed entirely in grey . . .'[42]

In 1844, they visited Scotland again. This time they travelled in the new royal yacht, the *Victoria and Albert*, on the building of which the Prince had had discussions immediately on the return from the previous trip. Again they travelled up the east coast, landing at Dundee, and drove the 50 miles to Blair Castle, where

JUST KILTED.—A SCENE AT BLAIR ATHOL.

136 *Just Kilted – A Scene at Blair Athol.*
Punch September 1844.

Lord Glenlyon, later 6th Duke of Atholl, had moved out of the Castle into his factor's house.

The Queen's journal again reflects the Prince's enjoyment:

Albert in such delight; it is a happiness to see him, he is in such spirits . . . a splendid view of the hills before us, so rural and romantic, so unlike our *Windsor* walk (delightful as that is); and this change does such good: as Albert observes, it refreshes one for a long time . . .[43]

The royal couple found Balmoral through Lord Aberdeen, whose bachelor brother had owned the lease, and it was commended to them by their physician Sir James Clark. He claimed that Deeside was one of the driest districts of Scotland, and Balmoral among the most favoured, with a sandy gravelly soil. The Queen and the Prince first saw it on September 8, 1848, and were so enchanted with it that they took steps to buy the freehold, such a complicated matter where Scottish trusts were concerned, that an Act of Parliament was needed. It was not till the autumn of 1852 that they entered the property as owners. On October 11, there took place one of their little ceremonies: the building of a cairn on Craig Gowan to mark their taking possession.

Sir Robert Gordon had rebuilt Balmoral Castle in the 1830s in the 'Scottish Baronial' style, first made fashionable by Abbotsford. This style, like the Gothic then fashionable in England, tended towards an easy going adaptation of Scottish external details such as gables and turrets to what was a basically domestic plan. Large Jacobethan windows and Tudor chimneys existed side by side with defensive slits and machicolated eaves.

Sir Robert Gordon employed John Smith, a London-trained member of an Aberdeen architectural family, who had contri-

137 Balmoral Castle from the opposite side
of the Dee, September 1857.

buted a number of public buildings to Aberdeen and executed
additions and extensions to a large number of nearby country
properties. The Queen and the Prince moved into Sir Robert
Gordon's house. John Smith prepared some designs for re-
modelling in 1848, possibly at the request of Lord Aberdeen, but
by the time that the house had been purchased the commission
passed to his son, William Smith of Aberdeen.[44] As at Osborne,
the Prince could have employed an architect of national standing, but he chose to turn to a good practical man. He was probably wise to have chosen an Aberdeen man, as many second-
home owners had run into difficulties through insufficient local
connections. But again one suspects the attraction was the
chance to see his own ideas executed.

In many ways, Balmoral is similar to Osborne. The planning
of the Castle has the same division between accommodation for
the family and guests, and a large service block. The original
house had been far too small as Lady Canning had observed: 'It
would be comfortable for a few people and a due proportion, but
now with *eight* at dinner every day, besides three children and
their governess, there are sixty servants . . .'[45] Even with the
enlarged Castle, there were still guests who had to be lodged in
cottages, as at Osborne.

Externally the Castle was built of dressed granite, a local
material but more expensive than the stuccoed brick of Osborne.
The Prince had not adopted the equally traditional rubble stone
'harled' in the Scottish manner used for much of the older house.

The provision of the ballroom reflected local conditions, and
the Prince provided for this purpose a temporary iron building,
of the type being exported to the colonies in Africa, before the
new house was started. When this was replaced by a permanent
room, it was sited next to the service block, underlining that it
was as much for the entertainment of the estate staff as the royal
guests. Though both the Queen and the Prince took lessons in
dancing reels, their English guests did not always learn Scottish
dances with the same enthusiasm as they had learnt minuets in

London for the royal Bal Costumé, in 1847.

Because Balmoral actually belonged to the Prince, and perhaps because of the resemblance to the mountains of Thuringia, the Castle is decorated with a number of Saxon heraldic crests, and the Prince's coat of arms is displayed over the grand entrance.

Internally, according to Lord Clarendon, the Royal Thistle of Scotland was more prominent. '. . . the curtains, the furniture, the carpets, the furniture [coverings] are all of different plaids, and the thistles are in such abundance that they would rejoice the heart of a donkey if they happened to *look like* his favourite repast which they don't . . .'[46] Later photographs of Balmoral certainly bear Lord Clarendon out but, if one looks at Robert's watercolour of the Prince's sitting-room, only the carpet is tartan; the light chintz curtains, the blond maple picture frames and the austere light furniture recall the Ehrenburg of his childhood, possibly even the Biedermeier interiors of the Burglasschlosse, in Coburg.

Life at Balmoral had the same contemporary mixture of royal business and royal recreation. The official boxes pursued the Queen north and, because of its isolation, Ministers at Balmoral lived even more cheek by jowl with the royal family. Greville, sent for to attend a Council to order a prayer for relief against the cholera epidemic of 1849, found himself kept a day longer at Balmoral because the horses had all been used taking the house party to the Highland gathering at Braemar. That evening while his Royal hosts practised their reels, he and the Prime Minister, Lord John Russell, played billiards to pass the time. He recorded that he had enjoyed the visit to the

Queen and the Prince in their Highland retreat where they appear to great advantage. The place is very pretty, the house is very small. They live there without any state whatever; they live not merely like private gentlefolks, small house, small rooms, small establishment . . . They live with the greatest of simplicity and ease. He shoots every morning, returns to luncheon, and then they walk and drive. She is running in and out of the house all day long, and often goes about alone, walks into the cottages, and sits down and chats with the old women . . .[47]

Other visitors were struck with the

joyous bustle in the morning when the Prince went out: the highland ponies and the dogs; the gillies and the pipers. Then the coming home – the Queen and her ladies going out to meet them, and the merry time afterwards; the torchlit sword dances on the green, and the servants' ball closing the day . . .[48]

Other visitors to Balmoral included the many royal relations, and it was indeed in the seclusion of Balmoral that the betrothal

138 *The Queen and Prince Consort Fording the Poll Tarf*, in October 1861. Engraved after the picture by Carl Haag in the Royal Collection. The picture shows the royal party returning from one of the Queen's great expeditions across a particularly deep ford. The Duke of Atholl, leads the Queen's pony with John Brown on the other side.

of the Princess Royal to Prince Frederick William of Prussia took place in 1855.

The following year Florence Nightingale was asked to Scotland, to stay not at Balmoral itself but at neighbouring Birkhall with Sir James Clark. From here she made several visits to Balmoral to expound the problems of the British army in the Crimea and to put forward her suggestions for reform. Through the intervention of the Queen and the Prince she met Lord Panmure, Secretary of State for War, a wealthy Scottish landowner and a former officer in the 79th Highlanders. Though a formidable antagonist, he was won over by the combination of Florence Nightingale and the royal couple. His promised assistance was not as immediate as could have been hoped and the struggle over the health of the British army was a long one; however, without such royal favour it would have been longer still.

Florence Nightingale, as she told a friend, was struck with the difference between the royal couple and those around them, whom she found more concerned with the inconveniences of court life. 'The Queen and Prince Albert's whole thoughts were about Europe, the Crimea War, etc. etc., – all things of importance.'[49]

The lure of the Highlands was, of course, country life, always an attraction for Prince Albert, opportunities for him to go deer-stalking, and for the Queen to sketch, sometimes under the tutelage of one of her drawing-masters, Edwin Landseer or Leitch. There were excursions and picnics, later, overnight trips called by the Queen in her journal 'Great Expeditions'. The Queen published a number of extracts from her Journal in 1868, *Leaves*

139 Stag shot by the Prince Consort.
Facsimile of a sketch by the Queen.
Engraved for *Leaves*.

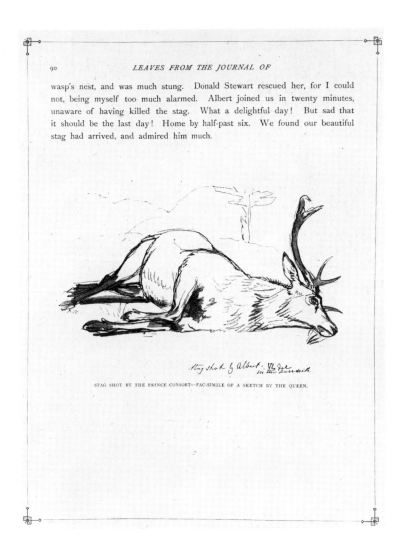

wasp's nest, and was much stung. Donald Stewart rescued her, for I could not, being myself too much alarmed. Albert joined us in twenty minutes, unaware of having killed the stag. What a delightful day! But sad that it should be the last day! Home by half-past six. We found our beautiful stag had arrived, and admired him much.

STAG SHOT BY THE PRINCE·CONSORT—FAC-SIMILE OF A SKETCH BY THE QUEEN.

from the Journal of Our life in the Highlands, and these give an attractive picture of life at Balmoral.

The children, as they grew up, were included in the excursions, and these events were recorded for the royal family, by their favourite artists. Edwin Landseer came to Balmoral on two successive years, and indeed painted the Queen on an earlier visit to Scotland. *Queen Victoria sketching at Loch Laggan* was a 'surprise picture' for the Prince at Christmas 1847. Roberts recorded the house, the Prince's sitting-room, and that of the Queen, on their visit in September 1857. His exquisite fresh watercolours were reproduced in due course as chromolithographs in *Leaves from the Journal of Our life in the Highlands*. Other pictures were engraved for the book, chiefly those by Carl Haag, some of which were painted for the Queen after the Prince's death in 1861. It was also illustrated with the Queen's own sketches.

Haag's picture *Fording the Poll Tarf* records the last 'Great

Expedition' made by the Queen and the Prince, a not inconsiderable effort involving some 120 miles mostly by carriage but a good deal of it on Highland ponies. Sometimes the going was so difficult that even the Queen had to walk. On the outward journey they visited the huts belonging to the Duchess of Bedford, at Clenfeshie, on the walls of which Landseer had painted a fresco of stags. On the return, escorted by the loyal Duke of Atholl and preceded by two of his pipers, they had forded the river. The Queen recorded in her diary: 'This was the pleasantest and most enjoyable expedition I *ever* made; and the recollection of it will always be most agreeable to me, and increase my wish to make more.'[50]

The estate at Balmoral offered even greater opportunities for improvement. The estate was neglected and the buildings ruinous, even by contemporary Highland standards. A programme of cottage building was embarked on, not only for direct employees, but also for tenants and for tradesmen,

the blacksmith, the carpenter, shoemaker, tailor and general merchant. Schools were built and maintained, a 500-volume library established for the use of the people living on the estate. To increase the comforts of his tenants, to elevate their moral and social conditions, objects steadily kept in view, from the time that the Prince became a proprietor of Highland property; and they were pursued with unabated zeal till the end of his life.[51]

140 Morning. The Queen, Prince and Royal family, ascending Loch-na-gar, engraved after a painting by Carl Haag. Engraved for *Leaves of a Journal of our Life in the Highlands*, published by the Queen in 1868.

141 Evening at Balmoral Old Castle. The stag brought home, after Carl Haag, again engraved for *Leaves*. There is a very attractive sketch by Carl Haag for the figure of the Prince in the Royal collections.

Right
142 The Duke Ernest II and Duchess of Coburg at the Rosenau, by Saleh.

Overleaf
143 Pages from one of the Royal Albums at Windsor Castle. Prince Albert in 1860.

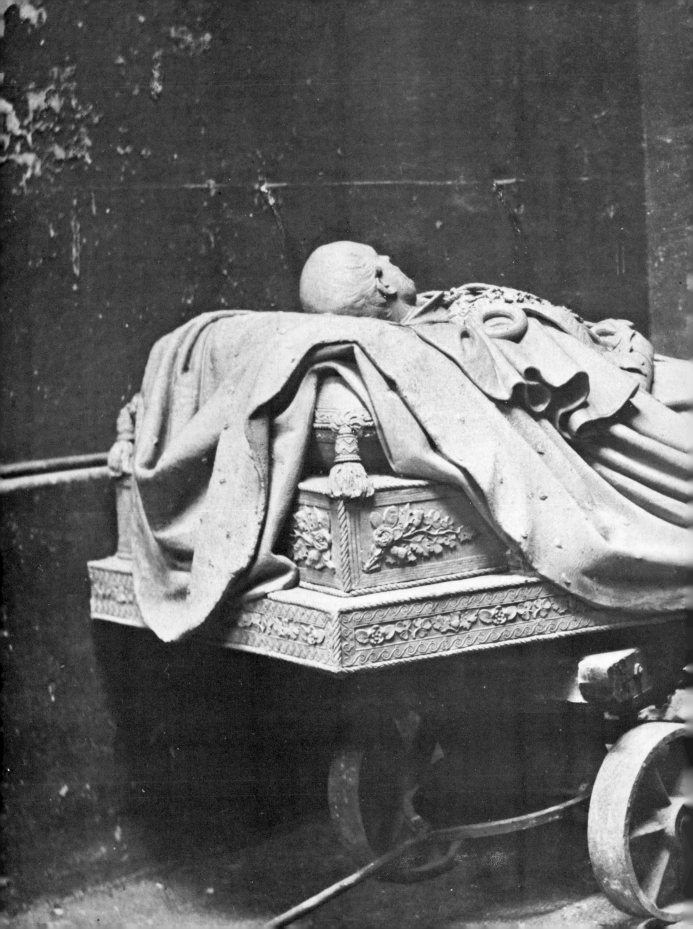

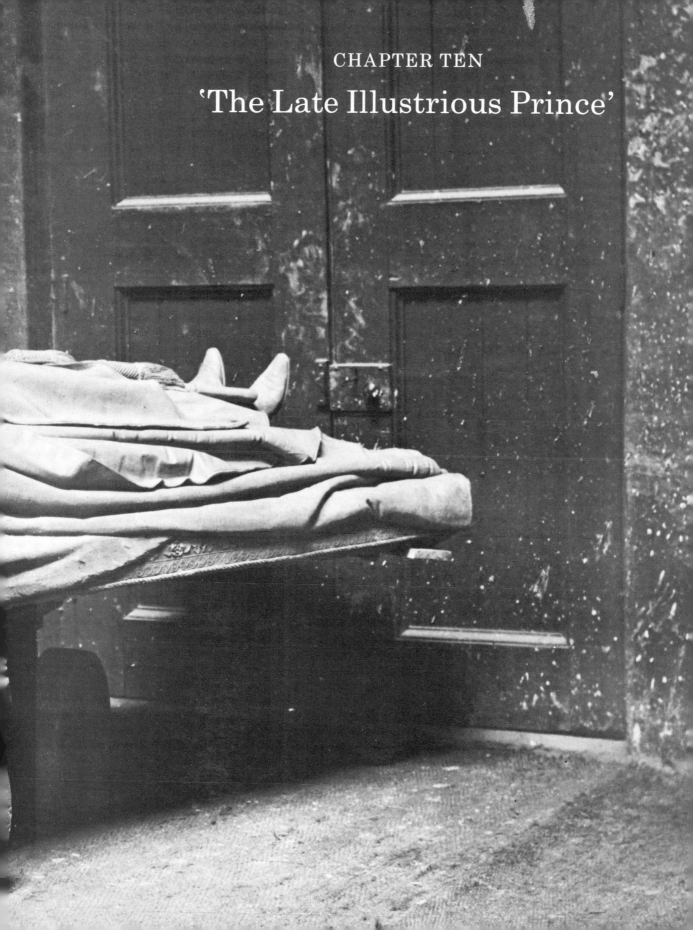

'The Late Illustrious Prince'

At midnight on Saturday, December 14, 1861, the booming of the great bell in St. Paul's Cathedral, told Londoners that something was gravely amiss. The following morning church bells tolled throughout the metropolis, but outside London many people heard the news of the Prince's death at church: his name was omitted from the prayer for the royal family. The news that the Prince was ill had been in the papers on December 9, but its seriousness was not made public until twenty-four hours before he died.[1]

The Prince had been ill for nearly a month with what was finally recognized as typhoid fever, then a dangerous and common disease, which had indeed just carried off two members of the Portuguese royal family. Prince Albert had, in fact, been a sick man for at least two years. His own diary provides evidence of increasingly frequent bouts of illness, persistent attacks of toothache, rheumatic pains, trouble with his delicate stomach, something which always attacked him when he was nervous before a major speech, but which appears more and more often in his diary, and the Queen's journal. In December 1860, he had had a bad attack of fever, the seriousness of which was concealed from the Queen, but which he described to Vicky as 'the real English cholera'.[2] An earlier illness had provoked a warning from old Stockmar, now permanently resident in Coburg:

. . . The unfortunate thing about your illness is, that while your position is constantly exposing you to the risk of having your health deranged, it makes it no less difficult to ensure the care that is required to restore it. All around you, there is a want of thoughtful care for the repose, the tending and the nursing which are so necessary for the sick and convalescent.[3]

This lack of proper care seems to have been due partly to the death of his valet, Cart. As the Queen wrote in her journal:

. . . Cart was with Albert from his seventh year. He was invaluable, well educated, thoroughly trustworthy, devoted to the Prince, the best of nurses, . . . a proud independent Swiss, who was quite a *homme de confiance*, and who might be trusted in anything. He was the only link my loved one had about him which connected him with his childhood, the only one with whom he could talk over old times . . . he was such a comfort to us, and now he is gone![4]

A further serious loss was the death, in February 1861, of the able young physician, Dr. Baly, in a suburban railway accident. He had replaced the septuagenarian, Sir James Clark, who had been the Queen's physician since her accession. After Baly's death, Sir James appears to have taken up his post again and, though the competent Dr. Jenner was also a member of the Household, it was Sir James who was in charge.

Whether the Prince's death was due to typhoid as contemporary diagnosis indicated or to more deep-seated disease, like

146 Prince Albert, at the age 24, by Thorburn. The Queen's favourite portrait of him.

renal failure or possibly cancer as some modern medical writers have suggested, his health was clearly damaged by overwork. He was a compulsive worker, a 'workaholic' in modern terms, partially overwhelmed by the growth in government business without a comparable growth in the royal Household's capacity to deal with the extra work.

The Prince seems to have found delegation difficult: thus in 1860, when the Prince of Wales made his successful trip to Canada, Albert added to his own burdens by drafting notes for the young Prince's speeches, something which was the province of the Secretary of State for the Colonies, Lord Newcastle. However, much of his work was highly confidential; as one newspaper put it, he was the 'twin heart' to the Queen, and it would have been difficult for anyone else to advise her on the proper reaction to the relentless flood of government papers.

These physical problems were made worse by worry and anxiety, and a generally depressed state of mind. Direct evidence of the latter is missing since his diary has disappeared, with the exception of extracts made after his death. His letters to Vicky make it clear how much he missed his favourite child, the only one whom he could treat as an intellectual equal.

His difficulties with Bertie are well known, though it is likely that, had his father lived, the two men might have settled down to an appreciation of each other as adults. All parents know the strain of acknowledging their grown-up children, and of being challenged by their young. The Prince of Wales was of course, in a peculiarly awkward position: biologically he challenged his father, in status he challenged his mother, who was by temperament much more jealous and emotional. He suffered all his life from the unhappy coincidence that his father's death came at a moment of extreme family tension generated by a stupid indiscretion on his own part. This enabled his mother to justify her natural jealousy of the Heir Apparent in a morbid reference to his father's death.[5]

1861 had brought more than its fair share of troubles for the Prince, but the worst was probably the death of the Duchess of Kent. This burdened him with the role of executor for a household never notable for its good housekeeping. Even worse, however, was the effect of her mother's death on the Queen, who seems to have had a nervous breakdown, thinly disguised by an extended period of Court mourning, which continued until after the annual visit to Balmoral. The result was that Prince Albert, in addition to his own heavy burdens, found himself supporting the Queen, deputizing for her in public, and devising entertainments like the 'Great Expeditions' from Balmoral to try and lift her heavy depression.

147 The Duchess of Kent, c.1859.

On returning from Balmoral, he found a new and acute cause of worry in Bertie's conduct. The Prince of Wales had attended an army camp at the Curragh during the previous summer, and had there formed a liaison with an actress called Nellie Clifden, an episode which had become the subject of gossip in the clubs. Having confirmed it, the Prince wrote to expostulate with his son, '. . . upon a subject which has caused me the greatest pain I have yet felt in this life'.[6]

Undoubtedly the Prince took the matter too seriously, partly because of his own ill-health. On the other hand he was only too well aware of the damage that a broken family life could do, and of the heredity on either side – of his wife's Hanoverian uncles, and his own brother's less spectacular infidelities. He saw such behaviour as a threat not only to Bertie's future happiness, but also to the standing of the throne. His own cautious and austere way of life had been designed partly to raise the moral standing of the royal family in the eyes of the public, something in which he had succeeded triumphantly. In this he was undoubtedly right, however extreme his attitude seems to modern eyes. In

addition, it seems likely that this incident has acquired an historical importance out of all proportion. Had it been one occurrence in a normal adolescence, later corrected by other events, then it would have become a mere ripple. As it was, the Queen saw it as the worry which killed 'the beloved Prince'. The 20-year-old Bertie found himself branded as the profligate son, whose behaviour had sent his infinitely worthier father to an early grave.

As Cecil Woodham-Smith has said:

> . . . The effect on the Prince Consort was catastrophic. He was unable to sleep, he lost faith and hope for his son and heir and with them his interest in life. 'I do not cling to life', he told the Queen. 'You do: but I set no store by it . . . I am sure if I had a severe illness I should give up at once, I should not struggle for life. I have no tenacity of life.'[7]

The following week he went to Sandhurst to inspect the new buildings for the Staff College, in which he took a great interest, coming back badly soaked and complaining of rheumatic pains. Despite this he felt it his duty to go and see his son at Cambridge on November 25, returning more exhausted and feverish to Windsor. So ill did he feel that he sent for Dr. Jenner, who was sufficiently concerned to stay the night at Windsor, but curiously, to modern eyes, does not seem to have prescribed any rest or proper nursing for his overtaxed patient.

To family worries was added the crisis over the 'Trent' affair, which meant increased worry, the coming and going of telegrams and Ministers.

The American Civil War had broken out in the summer of 1861, and the British government had proclaimed its neutrality on May 13, 1861, forbidding British subjects to enlist on either side. Though British public opinion was against slavery, the struggle was seen at first as being more about the right to secede. The Southern States sent two emissaries, Slidell and Mason, to explain their case to Lord (John) Russell, then Foreign Minister, who travelled on board a British merchantman, the *Trent*. This was stopped on November 8, 1861, by an American warship, which seized the envoys and took them off. When the news reached London, popular fury was almost out of control, while there was jubilation in America. Gladstone dined at Windsor on November 28, and discussed the 'American news'. The following day he returned to London for a Cabinet meeting, and then dined at Windsor, reporting to the Queen and the Prince on the discussions. On Sunday morning, December 1, the Prince rose at seven and worked on the Cabinet draft despatch from the British government to that of the United States. Though already softened and abridged in Cabinet from Lord Russell's original, this was still aggressive. Incredibly, the sick man drafted in his own hand

149 The draft memorandum written by the Prince for the Queen to send to the Foreign Secretary about the problem of the *Trent* case. It was during the American Civil War. An American warship had stopped the *Trent*, which was carrying two Southern envoys to Europe, and had taken the men off. The Prince's placatory wording probably prevented an Anglo-American conflict.

suggestions for a moderate reply. As the Queen later wrote on the filed draft despatch, '. . . This Draft was the last the beloved Prince ever wrote; he was very unwell at the time and when he brought it in to the Queen, he said, 'I could hardly hold my pen.'[8]

The Prince's ancient opponent, Palmerston, expressed his concern, and suggested that another medical opinion should be sought. The Queen's reply was that the Prince's 'feverish cold' should 'pass off' in a few days, a reaction which concealed considerable anxiety. Sir Charles Phipps, also in touch with the Prime Minister, explained the reasons for not calling in another doctor:

. . . everything connected with the subject requires much management. The Prince himself, when ill, is extremely depressed and low, and the

Queen becomes so nervous, and so easily alarmed, that the greatest caution is necessary. The suggestion . . . would frighten the Queen *very much*, and the Prince already is annoyed with the visits of the three that attend him . . .[9]

Two days later on Sunday, December 8, two more doctors were called in, and the following day a bulletin was sent to the papers, admitting that the Prince's illness was '. . . of a more serious nature than was first anticipated,' without, Phipps hoped, 'creating unnecessary alarm.'[10] Throughout that week the Prince's condition worsened: he became feverish and delirious, and generally weaker, but though the doctors were much concerned they thought they could detect some improvement.

On the Friday afternoon, December 13, 1861, the condition of the Prince could no longer be concealed from the Queen and, on her return from a brief walk, she was warned to expect the worst. A brief rally in the night cheered her, and deluded Phipps into sending an optimistic message to the Prime Minister. On that morning, when the Queen walked into the Blue Room where the sick Prince lay at seven in the morning she recalled:

. . . It was a bright morning; the sun just rising and shining brightly. The room had the sad look of night-watching, the candles burnt down to their sockets, the doctors looking anxious. I went in, and never can I forget how beautiful my darling looked lying there with his face lit up by the rising sun, his eyes unusually bright gazing as it were on unseen objects and not taking notice of me . . . Sir James was very hopeful, so was Dr. Jenner, and said it was a decided rally, but that they were all very anxious.[11]

The hope was short-lived. The Queen went out for a short walk on the terrace with Princess Alice, but returned to find the Prince worse. Through that long December afternoon his life ebbed away. The Queen waited beside the bed, the doctors comforting her as best they could. Five of the children were present, only the youngest, Beatrice, remained outside. (Vicky was away in Germany, the invalid Leopold in the south of France and Affie abroad with his ship.) The Prince's breathing grew more rapid, he wandered and dozed, oblivious of his children and those around him. He asked for Charles Phipps, who came in and kissed his hand, as did other members of his Household.

Prince Albert died at ten minutes to eleven that night, peacefully, with his wife, and other members of the family, Sir Charles Phipps and other senior members of his Household, the Dean of Windsor and the doctors, and his valet Lohlein, all present. It was a serene and Christian death.

Phipps wrote that night to Palmerston:

. . . The Prince is dead. I hope I had sufficiently prepared you for the dreadful event which took place at ten minutes before eleven this night . . . The Queen though in an agony of grief, is perfectly collected,

150 The Blue Room at Windsor Castle, in which the Prince Consort died. From a photograph in the Royal Archives.

151 The last moments of the Prince Consort. A lithograph after the painting by an unknown artist, in the Wellcome Institute Library, London. This was an unauthorized representation and caused distress and anger in the Royal family. A contemporary broadsheet advertises the sale of popular versions of this, together with one of the marriage of the Prince of Wales.

and shows a self control that is quite extraordinary. Alas! she has not realised her loss . . . What will happen — where can she look for that support and assistance upon which she has leaned in the greatest and least questions of her life?[12]

Public reaction was shocked, ill-prepared for the fatal news, and uniformly complimentary, many recalling the criticism of the Prince of a few years earlier.

Even *The Times*, often a severe and pungent critic, was in no doubt:

. . . The nation has just sustained the greatest loss that could possibly have fallen upon it. Prince Albert . . . — this man, the very centre of our social system, the pillar of our state, is suddenly snatched from us . . . It is not merely a prominent figure that will be missed on public occasions; . . . it is the loss of a public man whose services to this country, though rendered neither in the field of battle nor in the arena of crowded assemblies, have yet been of inestimable value to this nation . . .[13]

For those who knew him well, the loss was incalculable. '. . . The most valuable life in the country has been taken,' Lord Granville wrote to the Governor-General of India, 'and the public are awakening to the value of the good and wise man who is gone. The loss to the country is great: to the Queen it is irreparable . . .'[14]

The Prince Consort was buried on December 23, 1861, at a private ceremony at Windsor. Though, as one of the papers observed, '. . . the honours were of a private character, yet they could not be divested of that melancholy grandeur which attends the obsequies of Princes . . .', it was decided that a State Funeral would not be appropriate. The Queen's nerves were giving cause for anxiety, and she indeed left for Osborne with the Princesses. Only male members of the family and the Household followed the coffin, no women being present as was then customary.

The various regiments with whom the Prince had been associated provided the guard of honour and lined the route. Nine mourning coaches and a royal carriage preceded the hearse, which was drawn by six horses. Following the hearse were four empty carriages, belonging to the Queen, the Prince of Wales, and the Duke and Duchess of Cambridge. The funeral procession within the Chapel consisted almost entirely of the Prince's Household and his relatives. Members of the government and the Diplomatic Corps were present but not involved in the ceremony. The coffin was lowered into the vault below the Chapel, after the service.

The intention was, however, not to leave the Prince's remains in the vault but to build a separate mausoleum. This the Queen put in hand within a week of the Prince's death. The Queen and the Prince decided early in their married life not to be buried in

Ceremonial.

On the Morning of MONDAY, December 23rd, 1861, the Remains of FIELD-MARSHAL HIS LATE ROYAL HIGHNESS THE PRINCE CONSORT, Husband of Her Most Excellent Majesty, Duke of Saxony, and Prince of Saxe-Coburg and Gotha, Knight of the Most Noble Order of the Garter, will be removed from Windsor Castle for Interment in the Royal Vault in St. George's Chapel, in the following order, shortly before Twelve o'clock.

A Guard of Honour of the Grenadier Guards, of which Regiment His late Royal Highness was Colonel, will mount at the entrance to the State Apartments of Windsor Castle.

A Mourning Coach, drawn by Four Horses, conveying Two Valets and two Jägers of His late Royal Highness, viz.: Mr. Lohlein, Mr. Mayet, Mr. C. Robertson, Mr. E. S. Cowley.

A Mourning Coach, drawn by Four Horses, conveying Mr. Ruland, Librarian, Mr. Meyer, Gentleman Rider, Mr. White, Solicitor to His late late Royal Highness, and Dr. Robertson, Commissioner at Balmoral.

152 Order of Funeral Procession, December 23, 1861. From the Royal Archives.

the 'tomb-house' created by George III for his family below St. George's Chapel. They were not the first of his descendants to eschew it, the Duke of Sussex had preferred the more up to date alternative of Kensal Green Cemetery.

In fact there were two mausolea built at Frogmore, one for the Duchess of Kent, the designs for which were supervised by the Prince, and the one in which he and the Queen lie, where the designs were inspired by him, but were provided by a team of designers all of whom had worked for him.

The first mausoleum to be built was the one for the Duchess

of Kent, and here there are Coburg and English precedents for a building with both decorative and funerary uses. At Claremont a Gothic summerhouse, designed by J. B. Papworth together with J. W. Hiort for Prince Leopold and Princess Charlotte, had been turned into a memorial after her early death, though Charlotte herself was buried at Windsor. Professor Winslow Ames has suggested that it was the Hawksmoor mausoleum at Castle Howard which particularly appealed to the Queen, as she said in her *Journal*, '. . . A very pretty little chapel, with an extremely airy vault, – not at all dreary – beneath . . . It is just the sort of thing, I wish one day to build for ourselves.'[15]

The Castle Howard mausoleum had become the precedent for that for the Duchess, the Prince noting in 1859 '. . . The temple to be erected over a vault . . . so constructed as to be capable of being used as a summer house in the garden, if the other purpose was given up. Mama was much pleased with this arrangement . . .'[16] The design was entrusted to Ludwig Gruner and to A. J. Humbert, an architect who restored Whippingham Church for the Prince, and may well have been responsible for the restoration of Barton Manor also. The result is a charming building, almost Beaux Arts in style, a little circular aedicule above with walls painted to resemble draperies to Gruner's design, and below a vault for the sarcophagus, all perched on the mound in Frogmore garden. The Duchess did not live to see the building completed, but it was well under way in the spring of 1861. Humbert's correspondence makes it clear that the contract, with the London firm of I'Anson, was behind. The rival attraction of Ascot Week for the workmen did not help, but the building was consecrated at the end of July, and the Duchess's remains removed in a private ceremony early in the morning.[17]

The larger mausoleum for the royal couple themselves is clearly based on the family mausoleum in Coburg, designed by Eberhardt in the 1850s.[18] On their visit in 1860, the Queen and the Prince visited it:

. . . we walked to the Mausoleum or Erbbgrabniss, which is in the churchyard, – such a pretty one in such a pretty position . . . We went into the pretty mausoleum, which had been erected by the whole family, after Albert's and Ernest's designs, carried out by the architect Eberhardt. It is in the Italian style; beautiful inside with a marble floor and marble altar in the Chapel. There are side galleries in which the sarcophagi are placed; dear Papa's and Albert's own mother's are already there; but the coffins have not been placed in them. It is beautiful and so cheerful . . .[19]

The Queen chose the site for the mausoleum within a week of the Prince's death, despite a countersuggestion from the Dean of Windsor that Wolsey's Tomb-House, to the east of St. George's Chapel, would be a suitable alternative. This chapel was in fact

153 The mausoleum in the Hofgarten at Coburg, designed for the Prince Consort's grandparents. From an engraving in the Kunstammlungen Veste Coburg.

154 The Duchess of Kent's mausoleum in the gardens at Frogmore, 1861. After a watercolour by W. Leitch.

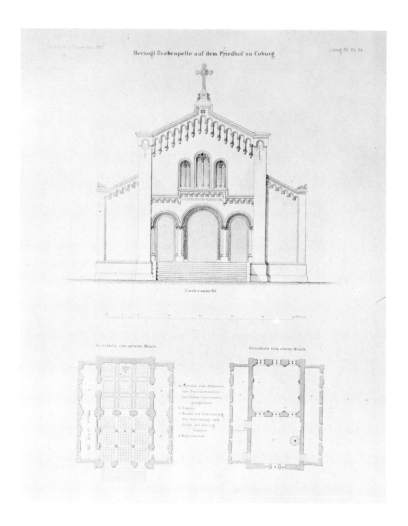

155 Designs for the Coburg mausoleum.

restored, and turned into the Albert Memorial Chapel, with an effigy of the Prince Consort by Triqueti, who designed much of the decorative work. Though the Queen employed Sir Gilbert Scott on the chapel, for the mausoleum she turned to Gruner and A. J. Humbert, with a new contractor George Dines, Cubitt's general foreman, who had taken over the business on his death. Also involved was Herr Ruland, another of the Prince's Household, doubtless because so much of the decoration was to be based on Raphael originals.

The plan of the mausoleum was to be a Roman cross, with the arms extended to provide an entrance porch and chapels on three sides. By the end of January the plan was approved, and on March 15, 1862, the Queen laid the foundation stone. In December the building was consecrated, and the Prince's remains were transferred from Windsor to the crypt on the 18th.

The exterior of the building is of Portland stone and granite, from many different parts of the British Isles. Inside, an equally varied selection of marble is used for decoration, much of it coming as gifts from foreign sovereigns. Thus the sarcophagus rests on a base of Belgian marble, promised by King Leopold, and the walls are of 'Emperor's Red' from Portugal, inlaid with other marbles from a wide variety of countries.[20]

Considerable problems were presented by the size of the sarcophagus, which was to be made out of a single flawless block of Aberdeen granite. Only at the fourth attempt was a sufficiently large block quarried at Cairngall in Aberdeenshire.

The recumbent effigies of the Queen and the Prince were the work of Baron Carlo Marochetti. Plaster casts were modelled first and that of the Prince was laid on the sarcophagus until the marble effigy was complete. The effigy of the Queen was not placed in the mausoleum until after her death.

The decorations of the mausoleum reiterate the Prince's interest in Raphael. Statues, bas reliefs and paintings are all based on compositions by Raphael, and many of them are carried by Nicola Consoni, who painted the panels for the Buckingham Palace ballroom. The original ceiling was a composition of gold stars on a blue ground, similar to that in the mausoleum at Coburg. Both the ceiling and the windows were renewed in 1901

156 Frogmore mausoleum under construction, March 8, 1864. From a photograph in the Royal Archives.

by Edward VII after Queen Victoria was buried there.

'How will the Queen bear it?' was the question asked yesterday by each of the thousands who, dismayed, felt that a national and individual loss had fallen on them.[21] This was the question which had occupied both the Cabinet and the royal Household during the grim hours when the prospects of the Prince's recovery gradually faded.

In wider questions she was to use the Prince's views as a guide for the rest of her life. '. . . Her Majesty considers it such a sacred duty to carry out every plan and wish of her beloved husband,' wrote Phipps in February 1862. This attitude was not altogether welcome to all her advisers; as Palmerston observed to Lord John Russell, the '. . . Queen's determination to conform to what she from time to time may persuade herself would have been at the moment the opinion of the late Prince Consort promises no end of difficulties for those who will have to advise her.'[22]

This approach can be seen in the personal context in her attitude to Bertie's smoking 'late at night', so bad for his intellect and his health, to Freemasonry, and in political matters, in her attitude to the Schleswig Holstein question.

More immediately she dedicated herself to commemorating the Prince in a number of ways — in putting in hand the family mausoleum, which they had already discussed, in having a number of statues erected, some at family expense, others by public subscription. The best known of these is of course, the Albert Memorial, but a large number were erected elsewhere in the kingdom, as well as a host of more practical commemorative institutes, hospitals and schools.

As they had commemorated their activities when he was alive with watercolours, photographs and sketches, so after his death she had her mourning, her daily life as his heartbroken widow, commemorated in photographs and pictures. One of the best known of these was the portrait by Graefle, of her in her widow's weeds with the Theed bust of the Prince Consort, but there were a number of others. Some were never completed, such as the *In Memoriam* portrait by Noel Paton. There were also a number of posthumous portraits of the Prince Consort, showing him enjoying favourite pursuits, like stalking, or in characteristic attitudes. These were often commissioned from artists who had known him in life, such as Carl Haag or Landseer, but were clearly based on photographs taken by Mayall and other royal photographers. Some of these were indeed photographs, carefully coloured and with the studio background replaced by landscape.

The most famous of these portraits is that of the Prince in armour as a Christian knight by Corbould, which in its turn

157 Portrait of Queen Victoria with the bust of the Prince Consort by Theed. From a painting by A. Graefle, 1864.

158 *Queen Victoria at Osborne* 1866 (also called *Sorrow*) by Sir Edwin Landseer. From the Royal Collection.

Opposite, top
xv The Aviary and Poultry Farm, Frogmore, April 1845. From a watercolour by C. R. Stanley. (Reproduced by gracious permission of H.M. the Queen.)

Opposite, bottom
xvi The Prince Consort's Sitting Room, Balmoral. From a watercolour by John Roberts, 1857. The clear cold colours and the blond wood are reminiscent of the Biedermeier apartments of his native Coburg.

inspired the Christening Cup designed for Prince Albert Victor, eldest child of the Prince of Wales. This is a reworking of the original Thorburn miniature of the Prince in armour, of 1844, of which the Queen had said: '. . . I cannot say how beautiful it is, nor how it exactly portrays the dear original . . .'[23]

Sometimes these pictures were conceived as deliberate contrasts, like the two Landseer portraits which she commissioned in 1865. Landseer was staying at Osborne to make sketches for a portrait of Princess Beatrice on her pony.

. . . Went to see Sir E Landseer making a sketch of the pony. Seized with a great wish that he should do 2 more chalk sketches, the one representing dearest Albert with a stag he had shot, at his feet, and I coming up in the distance, with one of the Children to look at it. Then the reverse of that bright happy time, as I am now, sad and lonely, seated on my pony, led by Brown, with a representation of Osborne and a dedication telling the present sad truth. Sir E Landseer is delighted at the idea and most ready to do it.[24]

There are two major statues which were really family mem-

159 The uncovering of the Prince Consort's statue at Balmoral, October 15, 1867.

Colour picture, previous page
xvii The new Ball Room at Buckingham Palace, June 17, 1856. The decoration of the room was based on Raffaellesque themes. Louis Haghe, *The New Ball Room.*

Opposite
xviii Design for the interior of the Frogmore Mausoleum, 1863. Watercolour by A. Croft, marked 'L. Gruner inv. 1862'. The Frogmore scheme is very reminiscent of the interior of the Coburg Family Mausoleum. (Reproduced by gracious permission of H.M. the Queen.)

orials, both by Theed, whom the Queen thought had caught the likeness of the 'beloved Prince'. Theed had taken a death mask of the Prince; though this was something of which the Queen was conscious that the Prince would have not approved. This was used for the Marochetti image in the Mausoleum, and also for the statue for the Prince in highland dress, and for that at Coburg.

The statue of the Prince in highland dress was executed twice, as well as a number of statuettes. It stands in the lower corridor at Balmoral, and a colossal version was erected on a Cairnlike base on a commanding position near the Castle. It was unveiled on October 15, 1867.

In June 1863 the Queen wrote to her Uncle:

... about the statue to be placed in the Marktplatz at Coburg, of my Angel, £700 has been subscribed by the people but £1200 are wanting to complete it. Vicky and Bertie have each given £200 – would you not kindly contribute £200 or £300 to this *dear* Monument? It would gratify me *much.* If so, may I know *where* to draw the money from? I will give the greatest part ... and the Model will be made here by Theed ... and the cast in Germany.[6]

The statue was unveiled on the anniversary of the Prince's birth in 1865. The Queen spent quite a long visit in Coburg, staying at the Rosenau, going for walks and long drives in the country, visiting the family mausoleum. All the children were present, the first time they had been together since Vicky's wedding in 1858. Vicky came from Berlin; Alfred, as befitted the Heir Presumptive to the Dukedom of Saxe-Coburg, had been staying with his Uncle Ernest; Alice came from Hesse-Darmstadt, where she was living with her husband, Grand Duke Louis of Hesse-Darmstadt. Even the delicate Leopold and the baby, Beatrice, were present. The only absent member of the family was King Leopold, then gravely ill with the malady which was to carry

160 The unveiling of the Prince Consort's statue in the Markplatz at Coburg, August 26, 1865.

him off before the end of the year. The people of Coburg united to do honour to the Prince.

The Queen bravely did the thing in style, bringing out the English royal carriages, and the postillions with their Ascot liveries, the first time they had been seen 'since my terrible misfortune, but I was anxious for *this* day to do all possible, and to do homage to my beloved one's memory.' She recorded the day in her *Journal*, finding it impossible to include it all but much moved. She told Uncle Leopold it was: '. . . The most beautiful Ceremony, I ever saw. Nothing ever was better done, and nothing was *more* felt. Sad and distressing as it was that you beloved Uncle could not be present. It would however, have been very trying for you.'[26]

Princess Helena described the occasion in some detail to Lady Biddulph:

. . . It was a beautiful day, not a cloud to be seen but the heat intense. We started off from here at half past 3 in open carriages with four horses and the postillions with the Ascot liveries . . . Grey and your husband met us outside the town in full dress on horseback . . .

The town was most beautifully decorated with flowers flags etc., the bells were ringing, the cannons firing; as we reached the Market Place, they gave such a hearty welcome, the band played the National Anthem, – such a crowd of people but they behaved so beautifully and showed *such loyalty* and sympathy. It was quite touching . . . The Burgomeister [gave] a beautiful address. Then the statue was uncovered, and such a cheer raised that it sent a thrill through us, and about 200 young ladies in white then put wreaths round the Monument while the Coburg March was played. After that the beautiful hymn of Luther was played (Ein Feste . . .] Then we all went down and put our nosegays round the Monument . . . I cannot tell you what a beautiful impressive ceremony it was . . .[27]

Prince Albert is one of the most commemorated of nineteenth-century English figures, his only real rivals being the Duke of Wellington and the Queen herself, distinguished company indeed. This outpouring of fossilized recognition was due partly to a desire to please the Queen, and partly through a feeling of guilt. 'We did not know until he was gone,' lamented the *Morning Star*, 'how much we prized and loved him.' The best known is of course, the London National Memorial in Hyde Park, the most complex and with the most impressive supporting sculpture, but there were memorials throughout the country taking various forms, not always to universal approval. Dickens wrote to John Leech, the cartoonist: 'If you should meet with an inaccessible cave anywhere in that neighbourhood, to which a hermit could retire from the memory of Prince Albert and testimonials to the same, pray let me know of it. We having nothing solitary and deep enough in this part of England.'[28]

The idea for a national memorial to the Prince was put forward at a meeting on January 14, 1862, at the Mansion House, by the Lord Mayor, William Cubitt, brother of the Royal builder. The meeting appointed a committee to raise funds for the Memorial, but in a tactful effort to spare the Queen the artistic wranglings which had been such a feature of the memorial to the 1851 Exhibition, the artistic direction was moved first to a smaller four-man Committee headed by Sir Charles Eastlake. Later the effective control passed to Charles Phipps and General Grey, both former members of the Prince's Household, and now members of the Queen's.

There were a number of ideas put forward. Cole wanted an Albert University, others favoured the idea of some utilitarian building, a notion which ultimately grew into the Albert Hall; there was a proposal to erect an obelisk on the site of the Great Exhibition. There was even an idea to build a sort of Valhalla, not only to the Prince but also to other national heroes, an idea

161 Competition design for the Albert Memorial, 1862, by P. C. Hardwick.

which had created the French Pantheon, and had found Germanic expression at Regensburg.

The proposal to erect an obelisk had to be abandoned since there was no quarry likely to produce a single piece of stone large enough, and this was tacitly acknowledged by the appointment, in May 1862, of a committee of seven architects, presided over by Sir William Tite. They represented the acknowledged leaders of the profession: T. L. Donaldson, better known as a Professor of Architecture; Sydney Smirke; James Pennethorne, who had himself worked for the Prince; M. D. Wyatt, who had been much involved in the Great Exhibition; George Gilbert Scott, best known and most orthodox of the Goths; and P. C. Hardwick, architect of a number of country houses and commercial buildings, and of the heroic Great Hall at Euston Station. Predictably, when the competition was announced only two names were added to those of the Committee, the two sons of the great Sir Charles Barry, Charles junior and E. M. Barry.

The designs were submitted early in 1863: many echoed the scheme of the Royal Horticultural Gardens standing some way to the south, with elaborate terraces and gardens; some included the proposed Great Hall favoured by Cole; and others, wanting a useful memorial, became a separate initiative, pursued by Cole and General Grey.

The designs were submitted to the Queen by Eastlake in February 1863, and she examined them at Windsor, together with the Princess Royal and Grey. Only two appealed, those of Scott and Hardwick, and she found the latter 'the only one that is really applicable', a predictable reaction because of the Prince's own preference for neo-classical style. The Queen thought that the other designs were too mausoleum-like in quality, something that would have challenged her own private memorial. She found the Scott design rather reminiscent of Kemp's Walter Scott Memorial in Edinburgh, and indeed of a market cross.

Scott had in fact deliberately derived inspiration from

the most touching monuments ever erected in this country to a Royal Consort – the exquisite 'Eleanor Crosses' . . . my next leading idea has been to give to this overshadowing structure the character of a vast *shrine*, enriching it with all the arts by which the character of *preciousness* can be imparted to an architectural design, and which it can be made to express the value of the object which it protects. The idea then, which I have worked out may be described as a colossal statue of the Prince placed beneath a vast or magnificent shrine or tabernacle, and surrounded by works of sculpture illustrating those arts or sciences which he fostered, and the great undertakings he originated.[29]

162 The Albert Memorial, Manchester, designed by Thomas Worthington, one of the earliest memorials to be erected.

In the event, Scott's design was chosen, according to Henry Cole, because of the influence of the Princess Royal. Doubtless Palmerston's advocacy of a Grecian temple containing a statue of the Prince could only have endeared the Gothic style to the Queen. The idea of a hall as part of the national tribute was abandoned.

The statue was to be surrounded by eight free-standing groups of statuary, representing the four continents – Asia (by John Foley), Europe (by Patrick McDowell), Africa (by William Theed) and America (by John Bell) – and four smaller groups representing the different categories of object in the Great Exhibition. These were Agriculture (by William Calder Marshall), Manufactures (by Henry Weekes), Commerce (by Hamo Thornycroft) and Engineering (by John Lawlor). These groups were not directly under the control of Scott, but were individually commissioned by the committee, though working on the general lines of Scott's design. Taken together with the carving on the podium itself, done on the site by sculptors for whom temporary studios were built round the monument, the Albert Memorial presented English sculptors with an unparalleled opportunity.

Benedict Read in his work, *Victorian Sculpture*, has pointed out that the Albert Memorial

for sheer size, scale, elaboration, and complexity, stood at the head of all commemorative monuments in Victorian England. The work's programme has been described as reflecting, symbolically but accurately, the Prince's sincere belief, under Providence, in the edifying role of the arts, the promise of advances through science and the benefits of material progress, and his adopted country's mission to spread these benefits to the four corners of the earth.[30]

163 Prince Albert's statue as Chancellor of Cambridge University, now at Madingley.

No undertaking of this magnitude involving such a diversity of interests and so open to public view and press comment could have gone entirely smoothly. The personalities involved were the touchy Scott, recently prostrated by Palmerston's interference with his design for the Foreign Office; the interfering Cole; the various sculptors and artists all jockeying for a prominent part in the most important commission in the country; and the politicians headed by the Chief Commissioner of Works, Ayrton, himself a cheese-paring Radical. Friction was inevitable.

Finance was already a problem, since the subscriptions had been disappointing, probably because of the economic recession caused by the American Civil war in the manufacturing districts of the north, and because of the number of local tributes to the Prince. Nonetheless, some £60,000 was raised and, in April 1863, a vote of £50,000, supported by the leaders of both parties, was voted by the House of Commons. In the event, the committee was given great assistance by John Kelk, a builder and developer with interests in South Kensington, who guaranteed his estimate of £85,000, by offering to pay any excess. He was a most appropriate choice as contractor, having been trained by Thomas Cubitt, and an ally of Cole's in South Kensington matters, but was treated with grave suspicion by Scott at first.

The choice of sculptor for the statue itself was a matter for the Queen, and from the first it was assumed that it would be the Baron Carlo Marochetti. He had modelled at least one bust of the Prince, and his statue of Richard I had been a notable feature of the 1851 Exhibition, and indeed of the Horticultural Gardens, until it had come to rest in Parliament Square in 1860. He was commissioned to make the effigy for Frogmore, though the Queen turned to Theed for the statue of the Prince in highland dress. But Marochetti died in 1867. The Committee then commissioned John Foley, already selected for one of the major groups of statuary. The bronze for the statue was contributed by the army, through the gift of redundant guns from Woolwich. This suitable tribute to one who interested himself to very good effect in army affairs did not pass unnoticed by Gladstone, who tried to prevent it on the grounds that the nation had already contributed £50,000, and no more should be provided.

The original intention had been for an obelisk with an equestrian statue in front of it. When Scott's design was accepted it was agreed that the Prince should be seated, though considerable concern was expressed over the problem of modelling a seated statue to be seen from below. One of Scott's own objections to an equestrian statue was that it would be militaristic and therefore clash with the concept of the Prince as the 'greatest personage in the country except the sovereign, and secondly, as the great promoter of art, science, and of social virtue in our

164 Prince Albert Memorial, Dublin, by J. H. Foley, 1871.

country.'[31] The completion of his statue was inevitably delayed by the death of Marochetti, which in fact enabled a model of it to be tried out in situ before the final casting.

The statue was finally unveiled on March 9, 1876, revealing the Prince sitting in Garter robes, holding the catalogue of the Great Exhibition, and contemplating the Albert Hall, and beyond it the Horticultural Gardens and the rest of his South Kensington dream. By then his reputation had suffered an eclipse from the unnatural high of 1862, and public interest in the Memorial and its statuary had diminished. The contrast between the gilded statue, and the tarnished surfaces of Scott's equally glowing memorial, did not help to raise it in public esteem.[32]

The design was criticized for its lack of originality. Nonetheless, it has gradually come to symbolize for the general public, more than any other single building, the whole Victorian age. It was in a sense a Victorian and not an Albertian building. Perhaps Prince Albert would, as Cole argued, have preferred an Albert University.

The Prince was commemorated throughout the country in a variety of different ways. Some of them involved quite simply adding a statue of the Prince to stand beside one of the Queen, as at Salford Park, where a statue by Matthew Noble joined one of the Queen unveiled by the Prince himself. The same thing happened at Leeds, where the Council solemnly approached the widowed Queen for permission to move her statue over to make room for one of the Prince.

Others were more elaborate, as at Manchester where Thomas Worthington's memorial was completed by 1867, and, like the London Memorial, showed the Prince in a Gothic shrine. A similar treatment was intended in Birmingham, but it was difficult to find a suitable site, so the completed statue – again by Matthew Noble – was placed in the Art Gallery in 1868, and then in the Council House. Both Dublin and Edinburgh achieved memorials: that in Dublin shows the Prince on a high base flanked by statues representing Science, Industry, Agriculture and the Arts. The same form was adopted at Edinburgh where the Prince's statue, by Steell, is surrounded by four free-standing groups all paying tribute, to symbolize those particularly indebted to him, including a military group, a farmer and his son and, perhaps ironically, a peer and his family. This monument was unveiled in 1876, and statues of the Prince continued to be made long after his death. There was a monument erected in Sydney, for which the Queen recommended a copy of Theed's statue at Coburg.

He is commemorated in a frock coat at Oxford, in a statue by Thomas Woolner of 1864, now in the University Museum. At

Cambridge, which owed him so much, Foley was commissioned to portray him in his Chancellor's robes, a statue which was placed proudly in the staircase hall of the Fitzwilliam Museum, in 1878. More recently the University authorities have seen fit to move the statue out — to Madingley, scene of one of the unhappier moments of the Prince's life, where, unprotected, it greens quietly by the lake.

The Albert Institute in Windsor, recently demolished, had a statue of the Prince in Garter Robes outside. The organization, which bought the site and re-developed it, has gone to the trouble of having the statue copied — even to the extent of the very curious representation of the Garter 'George', where the saint has been shown by the Italian sculptor as riding on a ram, rather than the more orthodox charger. It is worth noting that

Above
165 Prince Albert Memorial, by Thomas Woolner, 1864. Placed appropriately in the University Museum, Oxford.

Right
166 Prince Albert Memorial, Edinburgh, by Sir John Steel and others, unveiled 1876.

others seem to have found correct representations of military or knightly garb difficult: Francis Grant's portrait of the Prince at Christ's Hospital has been criticized for inaccurate uniform, while the Joseph Durham statue of the Prince in the robes of the Order of the Bath on the memorial to the 1851 Exhibition has earned the epithet 'Freely interpreted'.

Exeter recorded its gratitude to the Prince in an educational institute with a statue by a local sculptor, and other places also commemorated him in a practical manner with a hospital or infirmary, such as Bishop's Waltham.

Popular mourning items were produced in large quantities at the time of the Prince's death. Many of these were ephemeral, such as mourning cards and mourning ribbons produced by the Coventry weavers.[33] Most used representations of the Prince

H. R. H. PRINCE ALBERT
the projecter of the grand Exhibition of all nations. 1851.

167 Mourning ribbon. After the portrait of the Prince by William Ross. Such ribbons were made in Coventry.

already well known, including portraits and photographs by Mayall and other photographs.

Commemorative statuettes were issued. Other quality memorabilia were a series of Parian jugs, made by Minton in various sizes, carrying the arms and titles of the Prince. There are a number of commemorative plates but far fewer than at the time of the wedding 20 years before. The Prince's image was impressed on a number of boxes and useful knick-knacks. There is even a tape measure with the Prince's portrait on it.

Popular images included both photographs and engravings of the Prince himself, often after the Queen's carefully commissioned portraits, and also portraits of the mourning Queen. She herself was careful that the bust of the Prince should feature in group portraits, one of the most obvious being the occasion of her Golden Jubilee in 1887, when the bust of Prince Albert overlooks his matriarchal widow in the midst of his formidable host of descendants.

The most elaborate memento, and the one which probably catches the essence of the Prince's work most accurately, was the massive Tazza made for the Art Union of London, and issued in the year after his death. This was designed by John Leighton, and made by Copeland. The central portrait of the Prince is surrounded by representations of his various achievements, as Chancellor of 'An University', President of the Society of Arts, and Promoter of the United Arts. Round the rim runs the words from his speech to the Society for Improving the Condition of the Labouring Classes (May 18, 1848):

Depend upon it the interests of classes too often contrasted are identical, and it is only ignorance which prevents their uniting for each other's advantage. To dispel that ignorance to show how man can help man, notwithstanding the complicated state of civilised society, ought to be the aim of every philanthropic person.[34]

168 The Albert Commemoration Tazza,
designed by John Leighton, F.S.A., and
commissioned by the Art Union of London,
exhibited at the International Exhibition of
1862. As the *Illustrated London News*
pointed out to its readers: 'In the centre is a
medallion of Prince Albert, around which
are guardian angels, bearing views of the
three great Albert Edifices – the Palace of
the Legislature at Westminster, the island
palace home of Osborne, and the Palace of
Industry of all Nations, 1851.'

Acknowledgements

In writing this short sketch of Prince Albert's Life and Work, and in working on the Exhibition to which it relates, I have had the great privilege, and indeed pleasure, of working in the Royal Library at Windsor Castle and in the Royal Archives established by the Prince himself.

I wish to acknowledge the gracious permission of Her Majesty the Queen to use material from the Royal Archives, and to reproduce watercolours and photographs from the Royal Collections.

I am indebted to many members of the Royal Household for their generous help and the way in which they put their unparalleled knowledge of the Victorian period and the Royal Collections at my disposal. It would be impossible to mention them all; but this book would not have been possible without the help of Sir Oliver Millar, K.C.V.O., and Lady Millar, Sir Robin Mackworth Young, K.C.V.O., Mr. Geoffrey de Bellaigue, C.V.O., Mrs. Jane Roberts, Miss Jane Langton, and Miss Frances Dimond.

My researches in Coburg were made agreeable and fruitful by the help of a number of people, particularly Dr. Kruse and his colleagues of the Kunstsammlungen der Veste Coburg, Herr Oberender of the Staatsarchiv Coburg, Herr Jurgen Erdmann of the Landesbibliotek, Herr Auman of the Naturmuseum, Dr. Lorenz Seelig and his colleagues of the Bayerische Verwaltung der Stätlichen Schlössen, Gärten und Seen. I wish to acknowledge the help of His Serene Highness Prince Andreas of Coburg over a number of family questions. I am indebted to Herr Rudiger von Pezold, for a great deal of assistance, and also to Herr Herbert Appelsthauser, for giving me the benefit of his unrivalled knowledge of Coburg and its history.

I have received a great deal of help from members of the staff of the Victoria and Albert Museum, and again it would be impossible to mention everyone. Sir Roy Strong and Dr. Michael Darby, as members of the Organizing Committee, have given me special support, and help has also come from Dr. Shirley Bury, John Mallet, Dr. Peter Thornton, John Physick, Dr. C. M. Kauffmann, Julian Litten, and Liz Bonython. I am also indebted to the staff of the Museum of London, including Selina Fox and Amanda Herries; to Glennys Wilde of Birmingham Museum; to Julian Treuherz of the Manchester Art Gallery; to the Ironbridge Gorge Museum; to the Bristol Art Gallery; to the Welholme Galleries, Grimsby; and to the National Army Museum, Chelsea.

John Keegan, of the R.M.A., Sandhurst, and Dr. Huw Strachan have helped me over the Prince's contribution to the Army, Dr. J. S. Curl over the problem of philanthropic housing; and I must record a very particular debt of gratitude to Jeremy Maas for his generous support and advice over the Prince's interest in the arts. No study of Osborne House would be possible without the help of Mr. Sibbick of the DOE. My researches have been aided by the advice of the following who put their expertise and knowledge at my disposal: Tristan Jones, Steven Jackson, James Blewitt, John Bancroft, Christopher Wood, Mrs. Schwab, Stanley Cohen.

As always, I am indebted to American scholarship and generous help generally, particularly to Kip Forbes and the FORBES Magazine Collection, and to the Mellon Centre for British Art, Yale.

My thanks are due to my colleagues on the Organizing Committee and at the Royal College of Art, particularly Harriot Tennant, Joy Law, Griselda Kellie-Smith, Diane Smith, Finch Allibone and Francis Graham.

Finally, a very particular debt of gratitude is owed to my publisher, Penelope Hoare, and to Jeannie Chapel for her help over research.

Photographic Acknowledgements

I wish to acknowledge the gracious permission of Her Majesty the Queen to reproduce the following material from the Royal Collections:
Colour pictures: i, vii, viii, xi, xii, xiii, xiv, xv, xvi, xvii, xviii. Black and white pictures: 4, 5, 10, 14, 17, 18, 23–28, 33–42, 45, 51, 53, 58, 66–69, 70–72, 74, 76, 77, 87, 107, 116, 118, 120, 124, 125, 127–131, 133, 134, 137, 143–150, 152, 154, 156–160. Prelim pages viii and ix.

Bayerische Verwaltung der Staatlichen Schlossen, Garten und Seen: 81, 142. ii, v.
City of Bristol Art Gallery: 54.

Coburg: Prince of Coburg: 1. Kunstsammlungen. Veste Coburg: 2, 3, 7, 16, 153, 155. iii, iv. Prelim page xi. Landesbibliotek: 8.

Naturmuseum: 6.

Commissioners for 1851 Exhibition: 108.
Courtauld Institute of Art: 162–166.
Elton Collection, Ironbridge Gorge Museum: vi.
FORBES Magazine Collection, New York: 80.
Illustrated London News: 59, 63, 78, 92, 121, 123, 168.
Imperial College Archives: 60.
Jeremy Maas Esq.: 73. Prelim pages iv and v.
Manchester Art Gallery: 101. Also back cover.
Mellon Centre for British Art, Yale: 65.
Museum of London: 9, 19, 113. Prelim page vi.
Museum of Rural Life, Reading: 122.
National Army Museum: 48, 49, 52.
National Gallery of Ireland, Dublin: 98.
National Portrait Gallery: 13, 15, 22, 30, 31, 47, 62, 114, 135.
Courtesy Phillips Auctioneers: 20.
Private Collectors: 21, 29, 56, 119, 167.
Punch: 43, 46, 50, 55, 64, 75, 79, 91, 93, 102, 115, 117, 136.
Royal Academy: 83.
R.I.B.A. British Architectural Library: 161.
Library of Royal Society of Arts: 89.
Victoria and Albert Museum: 86, 90, 97, 105, 106, 109–12, 135.
Wellcome Institute Library, London: 151.
Westminster Public Library, London: 82, 84, 94, 132. ix.

Author's Collection: 11, 12, 32, 44, 48, 57, 61, 85, 88, 95, 96, 99, 100, 103, 126, 138–141. x. Prelim pages ii and iii.

Hermione Hobhouse
London. 1983

Notes

Introduction

1 Geffcken: Prince Albert, essay in *The British Empire* (1889), p 181.
2 H.M. Queen Victoria to the Crown Princess of Prussia, October 5, 1861.
3 Robert Rawlinson, friend of Jesse Hartley and George Elmes, speaking of Prince's visit to Liverpool in 1846, to open the Albert Dock, quoted Martin I, p 334, footnote 1.

Chapter 1

1 Dowager Duchess of Saxe-Coburg to Duchess of Kent, August 27, 1819, quoted Grey: *Early Years of the Prince Consort* (1867), p 10. (Henceforth referred to as *Grey*.)
2 Diary of Dowager Duchess of Saxe-Coburg, quoted Bolitho: *Albert the Good*, p 2.
3 Grey, quoting memo by the Queen, 1864, p 7.
4 Letter from Duchess Luise to Augusta Von Studnitz, quoted Bolitho: *Albert the Good*, p 3.
5 The Duchess Luise to Augusta Von Studnitz, quoted Bolitho, p 9.
6 Duchess Luise to Augusta Von Studnitz, quoted Bolitho, p 16.
7 Letter to Augusta Von Studnitz, quoted Bolitho, p 19.
8 Letter to Augusta Von Studnitz, quoted Bolitho, p 21.
9 Letter from Dowager Duchess of Gotha to Duke Ernest I, July 27, 1831, quoted Grey, p 8. Trans. different Bolitho, p 22.
10 Memo by H.M. Queen 1864, quoted Grey, p 8.
11 Quoted Grey, p 27 and passim.
12 *H.M. Journal* August 20, 1845, quoted Martin: *Life of the Prince Consort* (1875-80) Vol I, Chapter XIV, p 286. (Henceforth referred to as *Martin*.)
13 *H.M. Journal* August 26, 1845, quoted Martin: Vol I, Chapter XIV, p 291.
14 Mensdorff, quoted Grey, p 57-8.
15 Florschutz, quoted Grey, p 103.
16 Mensdorff, quoted Grey, p 59.
17 Florschutz, quoted Grey, p 27.
18 Grey, p 95.
19 See timetable printed in Grey, p 107.
20 Extract from *Gothaistche Zeitung*, Grey, p 400, Appendix B, April 13, 1835.
21 Letter of King Leopold of the Belgians, Appendix A in Grey, p 373.
22 Memo by the Queen 1864, quoted Grey, p 17. The Dowager Duchess visited her daughter and the little princess during September 1825 at Claremont (Grey, p 392).

23 Quoted Bryant: *Age of Elegance*, p 368.
24 Quoted Bolitho: *Albert the Good*, p 6.
25 Reminiscences of King Leopold, Appendix A in Grey, p 389. After he became King of the Belgians, he did marry Louise d'Orleans.
26 RA 45340-1: Duke of Kent to Baron de Mallet, January 26, 1819, quoted Cecil Woodham-Smith *Queen Victoria Her Life and Times* Vol I (1972), p 18. (Henceforth referred to as *Woodham-Smith*.)
27 RA/M3/3: Duke of Kent to Dowager Duchess of Coburg, May 24, 1819, quoted Woodham-Smith, p 30.
28 Hansard: July 3, 1820, Vol 2, pp 143 seq. Quoted Woodham-Smith.
29 Woodham-Smith, p 143.
30 Earl Grey to Stockmar: quoted Martin II, p 555.
31 Granville to Canning, December 16, 1861. Ld. E. Fitzmaurice: *Life of Second Earl Granville* (1905), Vol II, p 404.
32 Dowager Duchess to Duchess of Kent, August 11, 1821, quoted Grey, p 19.
33 Queen Victoria to King Leopold, June 7, 1836. *Letters 1837-61.* Ed Benson & Esher, Vol I, p 49.
34 Note by Prince Albert made in 1841 on RA/MA/57, quoted Woodham-Smith, p 122.
35 Queen Victoria to King Leopold, July 15, 1839. RA Y89/41, quoted Woodham-Smith, p 163.
36 Prince Albert to Duchess of Coburg, June 30, 1836, quoted Grey, p 135.
37 Prince Albert to Duchess of Coburg, August 15, 1836, quoted Grey, p 183.
38 Prince Albert to William von Lowenstein, October 26, 1838, quoted Grey, p 181.
39 Seymour's memorandum, quoted Grey p 194.
40 Prince Albert to William von Lowenstein, December 6, 1839, quoted Grey, p 246.

Chapter 2

1 H.M. The Queen: *Journal* October 10, 1839, quoted Grey, p 223.
2 H.M. The Queen: *Journal* October 14-15, 1839, quoted Woodham-Smith, p 184.
3 Prince Albert to grandmother, November 28, 1839, quoted Grey, p 244, p 424.
4 Prince Albert to Duchess of Saxe-Coburg and Gotha, quoted Grey, p 238.
5 Greville: November 28, 1839, *The Greville Memoirs*, ed. Lytton Strachey and Roger Fulford (1938), Vol 4, p 218. (Henceforth *Greville*.)

6 *A New Comic Song*, music sheet by C. Page Esq. John Phillips.
7 Quoted H.R.H. Duke of Gloucester: John Phillipsed: *Prince Albert and the Victorian Age* (1981), p 19.
8 *The Times*, February 10, 1840, p 4.
9 See RA Z293/9. King Leopold to Lord Melbourne.
10 Woodham-Smith, pp 194-6; Martin I, p 58 et seq.
11 Martin I, pp 60-63; Martin IV, p 63.
12 Greville: February 13, 1840, Vol 4, pp 239-41.
13 Prince Albert to William von Lowenstein, May 1840, quoted Grey, p 319.
14 Queen Victoria to Melbourne, quoted Woodham-Smith, p 222.
15 Woodham-Smith, p 215 and pp 228-32 passim.
16 Memo by the Queen, quoted Grey, pp 365-6.
17 *Punch* 1844: Vol 7, p 79.
18 Magnus: *King Edward VII* (1964), pp 19-20.
19 Lyttelton: *Correspondence* of Lady Lyttelton (1787-1870) (ed Wyndham 1912), pp 339 and passim.
20 Grey: p 366.
21 Greville: May 3, 1848, Vol 6, p 57.
22 Greville: June 16, 1845, Vol 5, p 219.
23 Queen Victoria to King Leopold, December 12, 1843, quoted *Letters* Vol I, p 510.

Chapter 3

1 Prince Albert to Stockmar: January 1854, quoted Martin II, pp 559-560.
2 Florence Nightingale to 'Clarkey', quoted Woodham-Smith: *Florence Nightingale*, p 383.
3 Prince Albert to Queen Victoria, December 10, 1839, quoted Grey, p 266.
4 Prince Albert to Melbourne: n.d. app./January 1840. RA Z273/12. Prince Albert to King Leopold: April 1840, quoted Blake: in Phillips: *Prince Albert and the Victorian Age*, p 31.
5 C. B. Phipps to Prince Albert, October 17, 1857, 1851 Commission Archives RC VIII. 105.
6 Martin: I, p 208.
7 See infra page 150: (X — p 273); also account of his death, Martin IV, p 280.
8 Greville: November 11, 1841, Vol 4, p 422.
9 Prince Albert to Duke of Wellington, April 6, 1850, quoted Martin II, pp 259-60.
10 Prince Albert to Duke Ernest: August 6, 1861. Prince Albert to Princess Royal: May 23, 1860. Quoted Martin V, p 109.
11 For details of his working day see Martin V, p 273.

12 Greville: 5, p 288, January 28, 1846. Lord George Bentinck: Speech in House of Commons, Friday, February 27/8, 1846. Hansard: quoted Martin I, p 321.
13 Greville: March 31, 1848, Vol 6, pp 44-5.
14 Lytton Strachey: Queen Victoria (1924) p 191.
15 Edward M. Spiers: *The Army and Society 1815-1914*, p 170.
16 RA Y.204. July 1843. 'The Prince concerts with the Duke of Wellington the abolition of duelling.' Martin I, pp 169-72. Christie: *The Transition from Aristocracy*, pp 127-30.
17 RA Y.204. September 31, 1843. W. Y. Carman: *The Albert Hat of 1843*. Article in *Journal of Society for Army Historical Research* Vol LVI.
18 Dr. Huw Strachan: *The Origins of the 1855 Uniform Changes — an example of pre-Crimean-reform.* JS AHR Vol LV, pp 85-117.
19 Prince Albert to Duke of Wellington, November 5, 1847, Wellington Papers.
20 Queen Victoria to King Leopold, August 10, 1853. Quoted Martin II, p 497.
21 I am much indebted to Dr. Huw Strachan for a great deal of help in dealing with Prince Albert's contribution to the Army. The references are to his Thesis: *The Pre-Crimean Origins of Reform in the British Army* (Cambridge, 1976).
22 Prince Albert to Stockmar, December 8, 1859, quoted Martin IV, p 509.
23 Prince Albert to Stockmar, August 21, 1860, quoted Martin V, p 173.
24 Prince Albert to Duke Ernest II of Saxe-Coburg-Gotha, May 13, 1860. Quoted *Prince Consort and His Brother*, p 206.
25 Speech on 200th Anniversary of the Formation of the Grenadier Guards, June 16, 1860. *Principal Speeches of HRH Prince Consort*, 1862, p 238.
26 Spiers op. cit., p 152.

Chapter 4

1 Martin IV, p 7.
2 See his speech to Merchant Taylors Company, *Speeches*, p 103-4.
3 See RA D/20 passim.
4 For Society for Improving Condition of Working Classes. See John N. Tarn: *Working Class Housing in 19th Century Britain* (London 1971) also Dr. James S. Curl *Thesis on Henry Roberts Architect* (London 1981).
5 Information from Miss J. Langton of Royal Archives. Prince Consort Cottages are still standing — see R. Carden *Meeting of Prince Consort's Association*. Watercolour, Royal Library.

6 Prince Albert to Duke Ernest, June 21, 1855 – Bolitho: *The Prince Consort and His Brother*, p 156.
7 Memo, quoted Martin IV, p 3.
8 C. Woodham-Smith *Queen Victoria*, p 147.
9 Speech on opening of Conference on National Education, *Speeches*, pp 185–6.
10 Memo by P.A., October 28, 1855, RAM 54/9.
11 Speech at Laying of Stone for Midland Institute, Birmingham, *Speeches*, p 170.
12 'Prince Albert for Lord Mayor' *Punch*, March 1847, Vol 12, p 113.
13 P.A. to Dr. Philpott, quoted Martin II, p 116.
14 *The Examiner*, quoted Martin II, p 129.
15 See Prof. Chadwick, *Prince Albert as Vice Chancellor of Cambridge University* in John Phillips' *Prince Albert and the Victorian Age*, pp 1–16.
16 Shaw Lefevre to Lord Clarendon, August 2, 1849, RA D20/14.
17 P.A. to Sir R. Peel, August 21, 1849, RA D20/22.

Chapter 5

1 Martin I, p 60.
2 T. S. Cooper: *My Life* Vol II, p 293.
3 See Turner watercolour: *View of Coburg 1840*, BM.
4 Cooper op. cit. II, pp 57–75.
5 *The Memoirs of W. P. Frith, R.A.*, p 92.
6 Ames, Winslow: *Prince Albert and Victorian Taste*, p 142.
7 Davis, Frank: *Victorian Patrons of the Arts*, pp 20–25.
8 Mrs. Jameson: *Handbook to the Public Galleries in and around London* (1842).
9 RA. Y.204. December 1843, January 1844.
10 RA. Y.204. October 1843.
11 See Fig. No. 73.
12 *See* Ruland, Charles: *Notes on the Cartoons of Raphael, now in the South Kensington Museum* (London) 1866. Pamphlet by Moore, Morris: *HRH Prince Albert and the Apollo and Marsyas by Raphael*, Paris 1859.
13 Davis, op. cit., p 24.
14 *Quarterly Review*, 1862, Vol III (No. 221), p 196.
15 Prince Albert to Lady Bloomfield, December 20, 1860. Quoted Martin IV, p 15.
16 See Grey, pp 349–50; also Manson: *Sir Edwin Landseer* (1902), pp 103–15.
17 *Quarterly Review* Jan–April 1862, p 196. Anon. obituary.
18 Nicholas Temperley: *The Prince Consort, Champion of Music* (1961), pp 762–4.

19 See Martin I. Appendix A, pp 485–501.
20 Lyttelton, op. cit., pp 306–7.
21 See music in the Royal Music Library at the British Museum, which includes manuscript material by both Prince Albert and the Duchess of Kent.
22 Mendelssohn: letter to his mother, July 19, 1842, quoted Martin I, p 487.

Chapter 6

1 *The Times*, October 18, 1834, quoted M. H. Port: *Houses of Parliament*, Yale–London, 1976, p 23.
2 W. R. Hamilton: *Second Letter to the Earl of Elgin* on the propriety of adopting the Greek style of architecture in the construction of the New Houses of Parliament, 1836, quoted Port: op. cit., p 23.
3 Port: op. cit., p 269.
4 RA. Y.204. Prince's visit, October 3, 1841, quoted Martin I, p 120.
5 Richard Redgrave: *A Century of Painters* (1866) II, p 518.
6 Prince Albert to Peel, April 4, 1844, quoted Martin I, p 122.
7 Barry, PP 1843 (493) xxix Second Report, p 11, quoted Port: op. cit., p 233.
8 See T. S. R. Boase: on *Painting*, Port op. cit. The whole subject of the frescoes is dealt with in great detail in this section, and also by the author in *Journal of the Warburg and Courtauld Institutes* 1954, Vol 17, pp 319–59.
9 P.A. to Charles Eastlake, December 2, 1841, quoted Martin I, p 125.
10 Thomas Uwins, August 15, 1843, Martin I, p 168.
11 Entries in June 1843 in RA. Y.204.
12 Eastlake, July 22, 1843, quoted Martin I, pp 166–7.
13 Port: op. cit., pp 272–6.
14 Journal of the *Warburg and Courtauld Institute* (1954) Vol 17, p 357. In this article T. S. R. Boase treats the subject at length. The section (5) in Chapter XII of Port: *Houses of Parliament*, pp 268–81.
15 Redgrave: op. cit., pp 548–9.

Chapter 7

1 D. Hudson and Kenneth W. Luckhurst: *The Royal Society of Arts: 1754–1954* (1954), p 183.
2 See E. Bonython: *Henry Cole* (182) passim.
3 Hudson and Luckhurst: *The Royal Society of Arts 1854–1954* (1954), p 189.
4 Hudson and Luckhurst: op. cit. (1954), p 189.
5 Martin II, p 224. He first mentions the Society in 1849.

disregarding the Prince's earlier contacts.
6 Luckhurst: *The Story of Exhibitions* (1951), pp 70–82. Allwood: *The Great Exhibitions* (1977), p 12.
7 Francis Fuller's diary, R.S.A. Archives. Scott Russell Papers.
8 Henry Cole: *Fifty Years of Public Work* (1884), Vol I, quoted Luckhurst: *Exhibitions*, p 97.
9 Quoted p 199. Hudson and Luckhurst, op. cit.
10 C. B. Phipps to P.A. September 1849, quoted Martin II, p 227.
11 Prince Albert's *Speeches*: (1862), pp 110–12.
12 Ld. Granville to C. B. Phipps: March 8, 1850, quoted Martin II, p 224.
13 Prince Albert to Dowager Duchess of Gotha, Martin II, p 359.
14 P.A. to King of Prussia. *Letters*, p 176.
15 Van de Weyer to Martin, January 23, 1871. Quoted Martin II, p 226.
16 *H.M. Journal*, April 30, 1851.
17 *H.M. Journal*, May 1, 1851.
18 Art Journal Catalogue Dublin Exhibition (1853).
19 *H.M. Journal*: September 1853; I.L.N., September 1853.
20 P.A. to Lord Ellesmere, July 3, 1856, quoted Martin IV, p 35.
21 P.A. to Q.V., May 5, 1857, quoted Martin IV, pp 37–8.
22 See *Survey of London* Vol XXXVIII, Chapter IX, for the building history and other details of the Exhibition Building for the 1862 Exhibition.
23 See Art Journal Catalogue for 1862 Exhibition: J. B. Waring: *Masterpieces of Industrial Art . . .*

Chapter 8

1 *H.M. Journal*: quoted *The Great Exhibition Catalogue* (rev. 1964), p 25.
2 Phipps to Playfair, September 27, 1851. RC 1851/WA. VIII 60.

Chapter 9

1 P.A. to Chancellor Woods: 1846, RA C26/32 J. M. Crook and M. H. Pat: *History of the King's Works*. VI, p 290.
2 Stockmar Memo, RA M20/5.
3 Memo from The Honourable Charles Murray, November 21, 1841, RA M20/10.
4 Stockmar Memo: RA M20/5.
5 Stockmar Memo, January 1841, RA M20/5.
6 P.A. to Peel, November 2, 1841, RA M20/8. Martin I, p 158.
7 Stockmar Memo, RA M20/5.
8 Peel to P.A., RA M20/62, quoted Martin I, p 160.
9 Martin I, pp 253–4; Pound, p 202.
10 October 2, 1840, Lady Lyttelton: *Correspondence* (ed Wyndham), p 300.

11 P.A. to Duke Ernest I, August 2, 1840. Grey E.Y., p 357.
12 *King's Works* VI, p 393.
13 See Y 204.
14 Lyttelton, p 307. She found the hare-hunting very distressing, only her admiration for the Prince's other characteristics made her forgive him.
15 *Punch* 1845: Vol 8, p 59.
16 See Portraits in album by Keyl. Royal Library Windsor.
17 See his book. A. G. Dean: *Selected Designs for Country Residences* etc. (1867), Acc. No. 615, Plates 1, 8, 19, 20, 20a, 21.
18 E. J. Powell: History of Smithfield Club (1798–1900) (1900).
19 J. C. Morton: *The Prince Consort's Farms*: An Agricultural Memoir (1863) gives a comprehensive picture of the Prince as farmer. See also the records of the Royal Agricultural Society of England.
20 Speech to RASE, York, July 13, 1848. Speeches, p 92.
21 See Morton, op. cit., and Menzies: *The History of Windsor Great Park and Windsor Forest* (1864).
22 Queen Victoria to King Leopold of the Belgians, March 25, 1845, *Letters* (ed. Benson and Esher) 1908, Vol II, p 35.
23 Memo by Prince Albert, RA F21/53.
24 For Thomas Cubitt, see H. Hobhouse: *Thomas Cubitt: Master Builder* (1971).
25 G. E. Anson to Edward White, January 17, 1845, RA F51/73.
26 See H. R. Hitchcock: *Early Victorian Architecture in Britain*: I: 183.
27 *H.M. Journal*: May 12, 1845.
28 Summerson: *Life and Work of John Nash* (1980), p 182.
29 *King's Works* VI (1782–1851), p 286.
30 PRO Works 19/7 f. 2238.
31 Y.204. July 1842, March and April 1843, C. Smith: *Buckingham Palace*, p 54.
32 *King's Works* VI, p 289.
33 *Letters* II, pp 33–4. Queen Victoria to Sir Robert Peel.
34 Letter to *Builder*, October 3, 1846, p 471.
35 Leading Article *Builder*: August 28, 1847, p 405.
36 For details see Hobhouse: *Cubitt*, Chapter 19 passim.
37 For Buckingham Palace see Clifford Smith *Buckingham Palace* (1931); John Harris, Geoffrey de Bellaigue, Oliver Millar: *Buckingham Palace* (1968).
38 P.A. to Duke Ernest II, December 23, 1857, Bolitho: *Prince and his Brother*, p 180.
39 *H.M. Journal*: May 8, 1856, Letter to King Leopold. May 6, 1856, *Letters* III, p 190.
40 *Builder*: May 31, 1856, p 298.

41 *H.M. Journal*, September 1, 1842, quoted *Leaves from the Journal of Our Life in the Highlands* (1868).
42 Prince Albert to Charles Leiningen, quoted *Leaves*, p 23.
43 *H.M. Journal*: September 12, 1844. Quoted *Leaves*, p 33.
44 Colvin: *Dictionary of British Architects*, 1660–1840 (1978), p 762.
45 Lady Canning: (1848), quoted R. W. Clark, *Balmoral*, 1981, p 30.
46 Clarendon (1856), quoted *Balmoral*, p 56.
47 Greville: Vol 6, pp 185–6. September 15, 1849.
48 W. L. Leitch: quoted *Balmoral*, p 78.
49 Woodham-Smith: *Florence Nightingale*, p 270.
50 *H.M. Journal*: October 9, 1861, *Leaves*, p 166.
51 J. C. Morton: op. cit., p 56.

Chapter 10

1 *Morning Post*, December 16, 1861. Eastlake *Journals II*, pp 163–4.

2 Prince Albert to Crown Princess of Germany, December 11, 1860. Quoted Woodham-Smith, p 402.
3 Stockmar to Prince Albert, November 8, 1859, quoted Martin IV, p 501.
4 Martin IV, p 281.
5 See Queen Victoria to Crown Princess, January 18, 1862, RA Add mss U/16, quoted Magnus: *Edward VII*, p 53.
6 Prince Albert to Prince of Wales, November 16, 1861, RA Z141/94, quoted Woodham-Smith, p 416.
7 Woodham-Smith: *Queen Victoria*, p 417.
8 RA Q9/23. See Morley: *Gladstone*, Vol I, pp 707–8.
9 Palmerston to Phipps, December 10, 1861, quoted Martin V, p 435.
10 Sir Charles Phipps to Palmerston, December 6, 1861, quoted Woodham-Smith, p 424.
11 Martin V, pp 438–9.
12 Phipps to Palmerston. Palmerston Papers, quoted Woodham-Smith, p 430.

13 *The Times*: December 16, 1861.
14 Granville to Canning, December 16, 1861. Granville *Life* Vol I, p 404.
15 See Winslow Ames: *Prince Albert and Victorian Taste*, for a discussion of the background. *H.M. Journal* 1850, quoted Ames, p 112.
16 RA M10/73, quoted Ames, p 112.
17 See RA Windsor 1861, pp 332 et seq.
18 Prince Albert to Duke Ernest, February 17, 1846; September 17, 1851, quoted Bolitho: *Prince Consort and his Brother*.
19 *H.M. Journal*: September 28, 1860, quoted Martin V, p 34.
20 See *Guide to Frogmore Mausoleum* (2nd ed. 1968).
21 *Morning Post*, December 16, 1861.
22 Palmerston to Russell, quoted Bell: *Life of Palmerston*, II pp 298–9.
23 See Mark Girouard: *Return to Camelot* (1981), p 115.

24 *H.M. Journal*, May 6, 1865.
25 Queen Victoria to King Leopold, June 9, 1863. RA Y109/34. The metal for the Statue was given by the King of Prussia.
26 *H.M. Journal*, August 1865; Queen Victoria to King Leopold, August 21, 1865. RA Y114/29.
27 RA Addl. MSS A/22. Princess Helena to Lady Biddulph.
28 Quoted Benedict Read: *Victorian Sculpture* (1982), p 95.
29 *National Memorial to his Royal Highness*, p 378.
30 Read, op. cit., p 153.
31 Scott, quoted *Survey*, p 161.
32 For a detailed account of the building of the memorial, see *Survey of London*: Vol XXXVIII, Chapter X; Read op. cit. *passim*; and Stephen Bayley: *Albert Memorial* (1981).
33 See article by Michael Darby: *Victoria and Albert in Silk. Country Life*: March 6, 1969, pp 546, 549–50.
34 *Speeches*: pp 88–9.